What Has Archaeology to Do With Faith?

What Has Archaeology to Do With Faith?

Edited by
James H. Charlesworth
and Walter P. Weaver

Faith and Scholarship Colloquies

Trinity Press International   Philadelphia

First Published 1992

Trinity Press International
3725 Chestnut Street
Philadelphia, PA 19104

BS
621
. W45
1992
PAP

Cover design by Brian Preuss

Library of Congress Cataloging-in-Publication Data

What has archaeology to do with faith? / edited by James H.
Charlesworth and Walter P. Weaver
    p.   cm.
Includes bibliographical references and index.
ISBN 1-56338-038-2 (pbk.)
1. Bible—Antiquities. 2. Jews—History. 3. Palestine—
Antiquities. I. Charlesworth, James H. II. Weaver, Walter P.
BS621.W45   1992
220.9'3—dc20   92-5202
                                                    CIP

Printed in the United States of America

Contents

Contributors

JAMES H. CHARLESWORTH is George L. Collord Professor of New Testament Language and Literature at Princeton Theological Seminary and director of the Princeton Theological Seminary Dead Sea Scrolls Project.

J. MAXWELL MILLER is Professor of Old Testament at Candler School of Theology, Emory University, Atlanta, Georgia.

JAMES F. STRANGE is Professor in the Department of Religious Studies, University of South Florida, Tampa.

WALTER P. WEAVER is Chair of the Humanities Division and Department of Religion and Philosophy at Florida Southern College, Lakeland, and Pendergrass Professor of Religion.

W. WAITE WILLIS, JR., is Associate Professor of Religion and Philosophy at Florida Southern College, Lakeland.

Faith and Scholarship Colloquies

This series explores the boundaries where faith and academic study intersect. At these borders, the sharp edge of current biblical scholarship is allowed to cut theologically and pose its often challenging questions for traditional faith. The series includes contributions from leading scholars in contemporary biblical studies. As Christian faith seeks to send a word on target in our day, as powerful as those in the past, it needs to sharpen its perception and proclamation from honest and truthful insights in human knowledge, from first-century archaeology to modern linguistics.

Preface

The phrase "*biblical* archaeology" has assumed a puzzling character. Perhaps it was always enigmatic: How can there be an archaeology of a book? "Palestinian archaeology" or "Middle Eastern archaeology" might have sounded more natural. And yet there is something revealing in the expression "biblical archaeology." It stems from a time when archaeology was thought of as the handmaiden of theology, as something functioning in the service of faith's devotion to the Bible.

But now archaeology seems less the handmaiden of biblical theology than its unwilling mistress. We cannot really speak of a legal separation, much less of marriage and divorce; we should probably think rather of two figures dwelling uncomfortably under the same roof, or perhaps (with a more appropriate metaphor) in the same agrarian village.

The reasons for this odd circumstance lie in the past, in a time when French aristocratic heads were rolling and certain of the landed gentry in America were rousing a revolution. Both had caught some English diseases embodied in the extravagant notions of deists and rationalists like John Locke or Thomas Chubb.

Enlightenment ideas birthed a human revolution, giving rise to scientific reason and new political aspiration. Out of that same matrix came the impulse toward scientific reconstruction of the past, or as applied to the Bible, what we know as biblical criticism. Part of that movement was the application of archaeological methods to the biblical record—hence, "biblical archaeology." It was clearly driven by the interests of faith, even though it was methodologically a child of the Enlightenment.

Years ago the theologian Paul Tillich observed that Protestantism enacted great courage when it took unto itself the methods of criticism and subjected its own central authority (the Bible) to the most scathing questioning. Prostestantism's move is today universal (except perhaps in the most arcane fundamentalism, which still bars the door). Criticisms of one sort or another are everywhere present in the household of biblical studies. Among the members of the household is archaeology.

Some of the children, however, have gotten rebellious and wandered off on their own. It is easy enough for the parent—biblical theology—to tolerate the troddings of, say, textual criticism, for there the theological cost seems slender. Historical criticism too does not overbear, for all those parallels and pathways can be absorbed as means of illumination. The discomfort level rises somewhat with something like form criticism, for here the historicity of the text comes into play. Even so, the discipline is a literary one full of uncertainty and arguability. But now archaeology—well, that borders on the scientific, and unfortunately for theology, archaeology is not necessarily enlistable on the side of verification of the biblical record. The rebellious child seems, like all its scientific cousins, more devoted to the truth than to its parent.

And yet theology has never wanted for creativity when faced with a conundrum. It endures not by compulsive conquest—at least not since the Inquisition—but by quiet absorption. So if it is not possible to roll back the tide of criticism, then we must somehow roll with it. If it is not possible to spank the archaeological child into obeisance, then we must find a way to indulge him/her. If it is not possible to remove the once-invited critical guests, then we must mark off the limits of their authority. If it is not possible to isolate faith from the vagaries of free inquiry, then we must determine that faith itself enjoys a certitude which lies beyond those boundaries, or even itself compels free inquiry.

Such have been and continue to be some of the means of dealing with the issues posed by the bedding down together of biblical theology and its critical family, including archaeology. This is the subject addressed, broadly speaking, in the present volume. Each of the authors has a somewhat different agenda, of course, but fundamental questions about these relationships underlie all. Their importance speaks to anyone who thinks such questions have significance.

The four chapters presented here come from a symposium in April of 1990 at Florida Southern College in Lakeland, Florida. This particular gathering of critics was a part of an ongoing series of such symposia designed to pose the urgent issues of faith and history. The series makes no apology for probing the *theological* questions raised by the critical inquiries of the biblical specialists.

Certain persons need to be acknowledged for their support of these ongoing projects and in the preparation of this book. The President of Florida Southern, Robert A. Davis, has been a consistent friend of these symposia and made possible their continuance; we owe him our collective thanks. The Department of Religion at Florida Southern has sponsored the symposia with effectiveness and generous contribution of labor. The secretary of the department, Beverly Johnson, has typed the manuscripts with unstinting good grace. Missy Turbevillle, student assistant in the department, rendered splendid service in helping to compile the index. My colleague and friend, James H. Charlesworth, has not only contributed annually to the success of these symposia, but has given himself over to the co-editing and production of this and other volumes. I gladly acknowledge here his participation, without which these events could not have attained the stature they enjoy.

Walter P. Weaver

Chapter 1

Archaeology, Jesus, and Christian Faith

James H. Charlesworth

In the late sixties, when I lived in Jerusalem, archaeologists often told me that little evidence would ever be found of Jesus' time, or of the period from 20 to 70 C.E. The span of time was simply too short, especially in contrast to the ten centuries or more of Israelite history, in which to search for evidence of ancient Israel. They were wrong.

The archaeological finds from the time of Herod and the Roman occupation have been unexpected and astounding. The catastrophic events that culminated in the destruction of Jerusalem in 70 C.E. have proved to be our blessing. The Roman conflagration sealed, beneath ash and ashlars, bones of humans who lived during the period assigned to the Palestinian Jesus Movement. Cooking pots, lamps, coins, statues, weights, leather sandals, braided hair, combs, mirrors, inkwells, houses, walls, doorways, iron nails, benches, chairs, bathtubs, swimming pools, and other *realia* from that period now provide invaluable insights into what life was like there and then. Iron spearheads and arrowheads, twisted bones, crumbled walls, and thick layers of charred timbers

1

are palpable and poignant reminders of how a magnificent period in history met a violent end.

In some ways the unexpected discoveries are more revealing of life in Palestine before 70 C.E. than what the remains at Pompeii disclose of life in the Italian peninsular before 79 C.E. The evidence regarding life in Palestine is more extensive. It covers the entire land of Israel, from Caesarea Philippi and Gamla in the north to Masada and Avdat in the south. It is more prolonged—most notably from Herod's monumental buildings at Caesarea, Sebaste, Masada, Herodium, and Jerusalem beginning sometime after 30 B.C.E. to the devastation of Masada in 73 or 74 C.E.

The sensational, of course, can distort balanced judgment. At the outset we must report that no undeniable evidence has yet been found of Jesus or of the Palestinian Jesus Movement. How would we, as an example, methodologically be able to distinguish a house owned by a follower of Jesus from one owned by a follower of Hillel? The cross shaped mark on a wall in Herculaneum is an example of the difficulties we confront even with such spectacular evidence. Specialists on early Christian art and archaeology cannot decide if the mark in an upper room of the "Bicentenary House" was left from the cross-shaped backing once attached to some wall hanging, or whether it is a mark left from a Latin-type cross once used devotionally by a Christian living in this Italian village before 79 C.E. [1]

Balanced, critical judgment is therefore necessary. Archaeologists have unearthed some spectacular finds from biblical times, but the claims made for archaeology are sometimes unfortunate. One well-meaning journalist, reporting on my own research, announced that my work would help "shore up" the Bible. How reliable is this sad commentary on popular beliefs? How many Christians and Jews think that the Bible needs shoring up? My own work has never intended to strengthen the Bible or the claims made in it. I firmly believe that the Bible is able to withstand the attempts of those who miscast it and seek to strengthen it. It can survive those who mistakenly claim to save it, as it has withstood the acids of humanistic research and of intense historical criticism.

The misunderstanding of the purpose of archaeology attended its use in the nineteenth century. In 1870, the *Palestine Exploration Society* announced its founding with these words:

> The work proposed by the *Palestine Exploration Society* appeals to the religious sentiment of the Christian and the Jew... Its supreme importance is for the illustration and defense of the Bible. Modern skepticism assails the Bible at the point of reality, the question of fact. Hence whatever goes to verify the Bible history as real, in time, place and circumstances, is a refutation of unbelief....[2]

Archaeology is unfortunately placarded as an aspect of Jewish and Christian apologetics. But biblical archaeologists are not laboring to prove anything. To cast archaeologists in that role is to be deaf to what they might have to say and to distort what is heard.

I am frequently asked if archaeology has helped prove the accuracy and reliability of the biblical story. Without succumbing to polemics or the urge to launch into an extended lecture, I usually refrain from pointing out that biblical archaeologists are not laboring to prove anything. At the same time, I do admit that archaeology has been of inestimable service in helping us understand, for example, the message of the prophets and of Jesus.

Unfortunately, the assumption that archaeology is out to prove the Bible as true or believable is heralded spectacularly. The subtitle of one of the most popular books in Germany and in the English-speaking world is revealing: "Archaeology Confirms the Book of Books."[3] The *New International Dictionary of Biblical Archaeology* has been announced with the claim that archaeology "frequently corroborates the biblical record and always enriches our understanding of the biblical world." No notice is given of the ways archaeology has demonstrated inaccuracies in or problems with the biblical account of historical events.

A scholarly presentation of archaeology and its impact upon Christian faith obviously must be truthful and balanced. The biblical story of the conquest highlights the taking of Jericho by Joshua, but gives the glory to God. The Israelites do not attack the city with a massive army. They march around it, eventually make a loud noise, and the walls come falling down. This event is dated through historical records and excavations to sometime in the thirteen century B.C.E.

Was the city as massive and unconquerable as the biblical account indicates? The answer is impressive. Archaeologists, especially K. Kenyon, have illustrated that Jericho is one of the oldest cities in the world. How old is the oldest strata? It is difficult to discern, but there now lies exposed for the eye of all visitors to see one of the most ancient structures in the world—a pre-pottery neolithic tower dated to about 8000 B.C.E. Hence, in one excavation in the Holy Land, archaeologists reveal that a tower constructed by humans predates Bishop Usher's dating of the creation of the world by thousands of years.

Archaeologists have even more interesting news to report about Jericho. It was a destroyed city with none of its former glory or power when the Israelites crossed the Jordan River from the east. Joshua and the Hebrews did not conquer a city that appeared impregnable. Later ballads, legends, and stories credited God, not Joshua and the Israelites, with the conquest of Jericho. While biblical archaeologists have demonstrated that Jericho was a ruined city when the Hebrews entered the land, biblical scholars have pointed out how Israelite lore developed. Later generations of faithful Israelites looked up, as do visitors today, saw the remains of a massive city, and celebrated God's apparently incredible actions in history. The account is recited and rehearsed in early liturgical and cultic settings. The glory rightly is given to the awesome power of God.

Likewise, specific sites described in the New Testament have been examined objectively by archaeologists. While the pilgrim may be shown what some claim to be the exact spot in Bethlehem where Jesus was born, there is no archaeological evidence to substantiate their claim. Sites in Nazareth associated with the holy family and the imagined place of the annunciation by Gabriel to Mary are unconfirmed archaeologically. The traditional spots for the feeding of the 5000 and Jesus' Sermon on the Mount are archaeologically traceable back only to Byzantine times. No archaeological evidence has been found that enables us to trace these events back to the first century C.E.

The impressive synagogues in Capernaum, Chorazin, and Migdal do not date from Jesus' time. They are much later, dating from the third to fifth centuries. When we walk in and study these ruins, we are not in the synagogues where Jesus taught and worshiped.

The place called Peter in Galicanto is traditionally identified as the place where Jesus was imprisoned and flogged, and where Jesus saw Peter warming himself by the fire during his denial. Archaeological research has shown that where Jesus' wrists were allegedly flogged is where animals were hung to be butchered. His alleged "prison" was merely an ancient cistern. The apparent Roman house of Caiaphas was a medieval house in which medieval weights were found. Episodes in Jesus' life cannot therefore be verified by a house that postdates them by hundreds of years.

These are examples of some of the ways archaeology has not proven the accuracy of the biblical books. Before proceeding further, however, it is prudent to define "archaeology" and to ask about the purpose of biblical archaeology.

Archaeology is the "science of antiquity." The original Greek word was used from the time of Plato[4] to the end of classical literature. Josephus entitled his *Jewish Antiquities* *"Ioudaikes Archaiologias."* Modern scholars have reemployed the word to denote strictly the assessment of *realia* from antiquity (these include objects excavated or assuredly

dateable to the biblical period).[5] In the present study, I will
use "archaeology" in the broad sense; it includes not only the
assessment of *realia* but also the recovery of ancient writings
(whether written on leather, papyrus, pottery, stone, bone,
or other material).[6]

Biblical archaeology is a scientific, interdisciplinary
study of the remains of the people who lived in the land
during the period covered by the Bible, or roughly from the
time of Abraham in 1850 B.C.E. to the destruction of Jerusalem
and the erection of Aelio Capitolina following the defeat of
the pseudo-Messiah, Bar Kokhba, in 135 C.E. Archaeologists
study, *inter alia*, pots, coins, houses, bones of animals and
humans, and especially the writings humans have left or
hidden. Their task is to seek to understand what life was like
at a particular time, what problems or catastrophes changed
the lives of the inhabitants of a room, house, town, or city.
Archaeologists' purpose is "to reconstruct the conditions of
life in antiquity."[7]

In attempting to reconstruct the conditions of Jesus' life
and that of the Palestinian Jesus Movement, we have the later
and edited records in the gospels, Paul's letters, and Acts
1-12. Archaeologists can help us complement these sources
and allow us to comprehend what life was like back then and
over there. Especially significant are the ancient written
sources, like the Books of Enoch, and especially the Dead
Sea Scrolls, even though many of the latter were not
recovered by archaeologists. From these sources we learn
about the use and meaning of terms associated with Jesus
and sometimes used by him, but never defined by him. The
list of these words and concepts is long and impressive. It
includes, among others, the following: kingdom of God,
Messiah, Son of Man, paradise, living water, the end of time,
apocalypse, determinism or predestination, the origin of evil,
theodicy, Torah, purification, targumim, pesharim, the
heavens and the angels who descend to earth from them, and
hypostatic beings like Gabriel, Sophia, Word, and Voice. In

this sense archaeology is indispensable for theology and the search for a better understanding of Christian faith.

Against the distortionistic use of archaeology by fundamentalists and the backlash against it by so-called strict scientific archaeologists, P. R. S. Moorey, the Keeper of the Department of Antiquities, Ashmolean Museum, Oxford, rightly states:

> Archaeological evidence, as such, *proves* nothing about the Biblical tradition. It only offers a constant stream of fresh information on antiquity from which to reconstruct the societies of the lands of the Bible, before, during and after the times in which the text we have was written down.[8]

That means that biblical archaeology is not intended to prove or disprove the biblical record. Archaeology does not evolve from the presupposition that the Bible is weak and needs the support of modern scientific proofs.

Archaeology is an essential branch of biblical research. It has made an impact on the translation of the Old and New Testaments with the discovery of manuscripts of canonical books thousands of years older than those formerly used as the basis for modern translations. It has provided letters, deeds, marriage and land contracts, and other written data that help us understand words that appear only once or infrequently in the Hebrew or Greek Bible.

Archaeology has demonstrated that some of our prior assumptions were inaccurate. Since the size of the rooms in Capernaum during the time of Jesus could accommodate only about two dozen people, it is better to imagine Jesus speaking to that number of Jews and perhaps a few gentiles, and not to think about him in a large lecture hall that would accommodate hundreds of people.

Not only the public but many excellent New Testament scholars are confused by archaeological discoveries. They have never been to the land and seen the sun sparkle on the Sea of Galilee, or walked beside the sea and looked up to the snow-capped peak of Mt. Hermon, or climbed down into the

trenches dug into the remains of Herod's once-majestic
palace at Jericho, or ascended the Arbel, or relaxed in the hot
baths of Gadara, or sauntered through the ruins where the
Dead Sea Scrolls were composed and copied, or followed the
ancient line of the Qumran aqueduct westward, or sat inside
the caves in which some of the Dead Sea Scrolls were hidden
from the invading Roman armies.

For the public and some scholars, Jerusalem tends to be
a symbol and not a city with ruins that can be dated scientifi-
cally back over 3,000 years. For them the Bible is a collection
of imaginative stories, beautiful psalms or prayers, and
penetrating theological works. But for biblical scholars, the
Bible is actually something much more; it is a historical
account of praise and reflection on events that disclosed to
the authors and their communities that God had acted in this
land. For such scholars, archaeology forces reflection on
what is the relation between the deposits of history exposed
in an excavation and the recitations of history edited in the
Bible.

The problems that are encountered arouse intellectual
curiosity and enliven reflections on the origin and essence of
Christian faith. The data now appearing from ancient Israel
are so numerous that they overwhelm both the initiate and
the expert. Perhaps it would be useful to clarify the different
levels of these discoveries.

Let me suggest three categories that will help us better
understand the archaeological discoveries of Jewish life
described by the gospels and Acts. (1) The tertiary level of
archaeological evidence pertains to the *background* of the
lives of Jesus and his earliest followers. Anything dating
from his and their time helps us to understand their lives. We
can now, for example, walk down (or near) the massive
Roman, stoned first-century streets they, or at least their
contemporaries, walked on as they went up to the Temple.
We can enter first-century Jewish dwellings and see the jars
in which grain is still stored, and pick up the weights by
which commodities were judged. Such evidence is essential

as we attempt to reconstruct the society and sociological milieu of Jesus and his followers.

(2) The secondary level of archaeological evidence describes the *foreground* of the lives of Jesus and his earliest followers. Anything that relates with some probability to the life of Jesus or his followers is not merely background to their lives. It is evidence of their own particular lives. The singular example of foreground is the apparent discovery of Peter's house in Capernaum. Here are found fishhooks and evidence of life clearly dating from the first century C.E., and earlier. The walls are too thin to support tiled roofs, as in Jerusalem, Pompeii, and elsewhere. The roof would have to be thatched, precisely as described in Mark's account of the paralytic who was lowered down to Jesus from the hole made in the roof of the house by his friends (Mark 2:1-12).[9]

We are left with questions: Is this the house in which Peter lived and Jesus taught? Is this the dwelling in which Jesus healed Peter's mother-in-law? Is this the house where the masses crowded around from the countryside, bringing sick to be healed by him?

(3) The primary level of archaeological data is ostensibly *data from* some period in the life of Jesus. The evidence of where he was crucified is the best example of this level. I have attempted to show in *Jesus Within Judaism*,[10] that the Church of the Holy Sepulchre is probably the cite on which Jesus was crucified. The massive white stone that can still be seen rising high above the floor of the church is a cracked rock rejected by stone masons who were quarrying stones in the seventh or eighth centuries B.C.E. This is the only site revered before the last century as the place of Jesus' crucifixion; and archaeological evidence that it was the traditional site of his death has been found dating back prior the fourth century. Since this place directly relates to Jesus' own life, it is not merely background or foreground.

Since the late sixties, we have obtained impressive evidence of the background and foreground of the Palestinian Jesus Movement. Perhaps we have also direct evidence pertaining to episodes in the lives of Jesus or his followers. The data has almost always been at the background level, allowing us to see, feel, and comprehend *realia* from that time and that place.

The lives of people important for a perception of Christian origins are now brought out of the shadows. Pontius Pilate is not merely a mysterious person in the gospels and the Apostles' Creed. His sinister personality is clarified by Philo of Alexandria, a contemporary of Jesus. His name and his title have been found chiseled on a stone in Caesarea.[11] We now know he was not a procurator, but a prefect.

Herod's personality springs to life, not primarily from the accounts in the gospels and Josephus. He was ancient Palestine's greatest builder, as we know from the remains of the cities he built at Caesarea (which still shows traces of his gigantic artificial harbor) and Sebaste, from the unparalleled grandeur of the Temple mount, and from the mountain he built in the desert at the Herodium, the only site to which he gave his own name. He was also a devotee of the sumptuous life, as we can now see when we examine his opulent palaces at Jericho and Masada, and the lower palace, monumental building, expansive swimming pool with pavilion and formal gardens at the Herodium.[12] The grandeur of the latter is unparalleled in the history of Judaism, is reminiscent of Hadrian's Villa, and conjures up thoughts about the lives of Jews who were taxed excessively in order to provide such luxuries for Herod and his elite group.

The recent discovery of a first-century "fishing vessel"[13] in the mud of Galilee helps us reconstruct the lives of fishermen during the time of Jesus. The boat would have held approximately fifteen men, four of whom would be rowers. Its depth is shallow; it is only 4.5 feet deep, although its length is 26.5 feet. The shallow depth would indicate that during storms waves would wash over and into the boat. We are provided with precious data for reconstructing the lives of Jesus and his disciples, at least thirteen men, who on more than one occasion, precisely at the time and place represented by the Galilean boat, were confronted with a vessel rapidly filling with water as waves splashed over the sides. The inferior timber, old parts reused in the construction of the vessel, and the recurrent repairs witness to the low economic level of some first-century Galileans. Perhaps another dimension is thereby given to Jesus' association with the poor. In any case, we need to think more about the economic conditions of first-century Galileans.

Archaeologists have reminded us of the religious life of first-century Palestinian Jews. We can study first-century synagogues at Gamla, the Herodium, and Masada in which the earliest Jewish statutory prayers, now preserved in the Mishnah, were recited and in which the Davidic Psalms and other works were used liturgically. Moreover, the discovery of early Jewish hymnbooks—the Psalms of Solomon, the Hodayoth, the Qumran Psalm Scroll, and other compositions like the Qumran Pseudepigraphic Hymns and the Psalms of the Sabbath Sacrifice—help us comprehend the deep piety, cosmic dimensions of worship, and creativity of Jews roughly contemporaneous with Jesus.

Archaeologists, however, have also confronted us with disturbing reminders of Roman soldiers in the land. From Gamla to Masada we can bend over and examine the ballistic missles the Romans used to wreak destruction. Their iron spears and arrowheads have been found near human bones and deep in ashes—grim reminders of the conflagrations they brought to ancient Palestine.

Our consciousness of the pain, suffering, and destruction endured by Jews in Roman times has been jolted by the remains of the Burnt House in the upper city of Jerusalem.[14] Here was found the arm of a woman who did not make it out of the door when the house caught fire, probably from the Roman soldiers' incendiary torches in 70 C.E. [15] Here can be seen large wooden beams, charred areas, and thick deposits of black ash. The conflagration was so severe that the eastern wall of the house crashed westward. Surely these are poignant reminders of the struggle for survival not only of

Palestinian Jews around 70 C.E. but also of Jesus' contemporaries a few decades earlier. Their struggle, moreover, was also for the survival of ancient religious traditions; for the Burnt House was the home of a high priestly family called Bar Kitros, about whom we know about from rabbinic studies.

In this house we find reminders of two probable dimensions that help us understand Jesus' death forty years earlier. He was certainly put on the cross by the verdict of the Roman prefect, Pontius Pilate, and by Roman soldiers. Their attempts to keep some peace in the land are among the most colossal failures in antiquity.

We discover also the extreme provisions for purification devised by priests and other aristocrats. In the Burnt House are found massive stone vessels to protect against impurities of someone who might enter the house. According to the recently published Temple Scroll, a woman who was impure would contaminate everything in a house that was preserved in clay vessels.[16] Jesus' concept of purity was categorically different from the priests in Jerusalem and, according to the New Testament accounts, the priests, not the majority of Jews, were behind Jesus' arrest in the Garden of Gethsemane. In the Burnt House, then, we are confronted with clues and indicators regarding the background of Jesus and his earliest followers.

A spinoff of this archaeological research is a renewed appreciation of the historical veracity of Josephus's descriptions of topography and the Roman conquest from 66 to 73/74 C.E. Coins found in Sepphoris are dated to the period of the First Revolt. They bear the name Eirenopolis ("city for peace"), an apt description of the city in Galilee which, according to Josephus, did not support his resistance army but went over to the side of the Romans.

Josephus's descriptions of Gamla are astoundingly accurate, as anyone can perceive by standing on the cliff east of the ruins and reading his *War*. The Temple was indeed one of the wonders of the ancient world, precisely as Josephus stated. A stone in the western retaining wall of the Temple mount, for example, weighs well over 400 tons.

Another spinoff is an awareness that the Gospel of John is not simply a theological work that weaves together symbolical and nonhistorical ideas. Only John describes the Pool of Bethsaida, which has been unearthed precisely where he described it, just north of the Temple area. Only John mentions that *stone vessels* were set aside for the Jewish rites of purification.

Similarly, we now comprehend that Luke, the author of Luke and Acts, was not simply a theologian, as Conzelmann claimed in *The Theology of St Luke*. He was also a historian, and he wanted his readers to judge him as one who had mastered historiography. This intention is transparent to me after comparing Luke 1:1-4 with Polybius (especially Book 12) and from studying Luke's synchronisms.[17] His description of the central social importance of the Temple in Acts 1-12, for example, is precisely what we have come to comprehend was the social setting of Jews in Jerusalem when they periodically moved towards the Temple to worship and sacrifice. By studying archaeological discoveries in Jerusalem and reading Josephus and Acts, as well as some of the Pseudepigrapha and the Mishnah, we can grasp that the Jerusalem of the Jesus Palestinian Movement was cosmopolitan and yet a city dominated by the Temple and its varied religious, and even secular, activities.

Archaeological discoveries that have opened our eyes to the biblical world have astounded many. They have been featured during the last four years on the CBS and NBC evening news programs, on morning talk shows, and regularly in the *New York Times, Newsweek, Time, Southern Living*, and the *U.S. News and World Report*. These discoveries have also been reported in many other widely read newspapers and magazines, and by the UPI, AP, Knight-Rider, and other syndicated news agencies.

Two silver amulets, written in the oldest form of Hebrew writing (paleo-Hebrew), have been found in a tomb on the west shoulder of the Hinnom Valley protected under the debris of a fallen roof.[18]

Each contains the Aaronic Benediction preserved in Num. 6:24-26 and still recited today in synagogues and churches throughout the world:

> The Lord bless you and keep you.
> The Lord make his face shine upon you,
> and be gracious unto you.
> The Lord lift up his countenance upon you,
> and give you peace.

These texts predate the destruction of Jerusalem by the Babylonians, 597 B.C.E. They date to about 600 B.C.E., and thus antedate the biblical manuscripts found among the Dead Sea Scrolls by about 300 years. These texts, in fact, own pride of place as the oldest biblical texts in the world.

An ivory pomegranate has also been recovered—tiny and fragile—containing, in paleo-Hebrew, the name of Yahweh.[19] It is the only object extant from Solomon's Temple. These discoveries are truly sensational, and they show little sign of abating. But what has all of this *realia* to do with faith?

Archaeologists have provided even more startling discoveries that have thrown open windows through which we can see the settings of the lives of Jesus' contemporaries. The ruins of olive presses, elegant homes, impressive streets, massive walls, a fallen tower, a synagogue, and Roman ballistic missiles have been recovered from Gamla.[20] It is easy to imagine the final days of this Galilean city and the episodes that Josephus describes so poignantly as occurring in 67 C.E.: the fall of the tower; the breach in the wall; the collapsing roofs; and finally, the suicides of children, women, and men who threw themselves from the citadel, choosing death over capture and torture by pagan soldiers.

The pre-Christian shrines at Caesarea Philippi, the earliest black basalt buildings at Chorazin, the small but elegant courtyards and houses at Caesarea, the high amphitheater and other early first-century structures at Sepphoris,[21] and the recovery of a first-century fishing boat near Magdala on the shore of the Sea of Galilee help us reconstruct the lives of Jews living in Galilee during Jesus' public ministry. The majestic palaces of Herod at Caesarea Maritima, Jericho, Masada, and the Herodium are matched only by the Roman emperor's villas in Italy. These guide our reconstructions of overtaxed landowners, rapidly becoming tenant farmers, and the opulence of the upper echelon in Jesus' day. Such notions are enhanced by the discovery of large halls, magnificent ritual baths (*mikvaoth*), and mosaic floors in the homes of the wealthy, many of whom were priests, in the upper city of Herodian Jerusalem.[22] Our ability to reconstruct those times is strengthened by the insights that come from immersing ourselves in the Roman and earlier ruins of that romantic city, Petra, built in the mountains and carved out of living stone, and thoughts of caravans moving spice, silk, and incense from the East and the South through Petra, Jerusalem, and Ashkelon or Joppa, to Athens and especially Rome.

Piles of Roman stone ballistic missiles at Gamla, some with signs of burning and perhaps of stained blood; layers of ash beneath Roman coins and amidst Roman arrowheads in a stratum of the ruins once occupied by the authors of the Dead Sea Scrolls; a skeleton arm from a woman who fell in the house of the high priestly family of Kitros amidst ample evidence of burning and destruction by the Romans in the upper city of Jerusalem in 70 C.E.; the plaited black hair of a young woman who died at the hands of her husband in 73 or 74 C.E. just before the Romans breached the walls of Masada—all these combine with other *realia* from the first century to help us understand Jesus' plaintiff call for remembrance, warnings against zealous rebellion, and the impending devastation of Jerusalem. We are forced to wonder what went wrong: why did the Romans not follow their high standards of justice and due process under the law? Why were such incompetents as Pontius Pilate and

Festus sent to govern Palestine? Why did the prefectors and procurators become increasingly corrupt and hostile to law-abiding Palestinian Jews? Why was Jesus crucified by the edict of a Roman governor and executed by Roman soldiers? Archaeologists have helped us raise these and related questions with fresh insight.

The preceding reflections help us grasp some ways that archaeology is not irrelevant for Christian faith. But is archaeology really germane to Christian faith?

In the introduction to his commentary on Paul's Epistle to the Romans, one of the great theologians of this century, Karl Barth, wrote the following:

> Paul, as a child of his age, addressed his contemporaries. It is, however, far more important that, as Prophet and Apostle of the Kingdom of God, he veritably speaks to all men of every age. The differences between then and now, there and here, no doubt require careful investigation and consideration. But the purpose of such investigation can only be to demonstrate that these differences are, in fact, purely trivial.[23]

These thoughts were crafted in a highly charged emotional and polemical context. Barth exhorted scholars and others to take seriously the theological context and content of the biblical record. For him, the historical study of the New Testament had replaced the theological discussion of the content. He won the battle by turning attention from purely historical concerns.[24] With Barth and others, including his frequent adversary Bultmann, virtually all of us would agree that we cannot build theological claims on historical judgments.

But Barth and others, including Bultmann, created another problem. They did not sufficiently emphasize that biblical theologians cannot treat cavalierly historical research. Archaeology must not be miscast as if it can confirm or invalidate a religious interpretation of history. Nevertheless, it is a *sine qua non* for assisting us in establishing the facts that have been so interpreted, and we must always begin with and give pride of place in reconstruction to the texts.[25] As many New Testament specialists have pointed out, only by taking historical research seriously is there any means of distinguishing illumination from illusion, and faith from fiction.

Today, in contrast to the days of Barth and Bultmann, historical research includes both the sociological investigation of Christian origins and the archaeological discussion and evidence of first-century Palestinian life. Previous generations of biblical scholars did not have the opportunity to perceive the exciting discoveries now available to us from lives lived out in Palestine before 70 C.E.

While archaeology will never lead to theology, nor ancient ashlars to confessional commitment, archaeology is essential to any who wish to know about the particularity of the Jewish and Christian confession that one God has acted decisively on our behalf through the Hebrews, Israelites, and Jews in specific places and in unique ways. Archaeology is a bulwark against the tide of modernizing Jesus, which is as dangerously prevalent in our day as it was in the time of Albert Schweitzer.[26] Archaeology and historical research are our only means for showing that Jesus was a faithful Palestinian Jew,[27] not a Zealot as Brandon claimed,[28] black revolutionary as Cleage argued,[29] or gentile as H. St. Chamberlain contended.[30]

Here, too, we must admit that even archaeology and historical research cannot alone perform the full task. Along with theological research and study, it can help us see that Jesus must not be portrayed as the-man-of-the-future, as J. Middleton Murry[31] contended, nor the divine propagandist, as Lord Beaverbrook[32] envisioned. These methodologies and areas of scholarship together help demonstrate that Jesus was not married, as William E. Phipps suggests,[33] or an illegitimate child, as Jane Schaberg claims.[34]

Obviously, then, archaeology has a powerful service to perform for theology and Christian faith, since Christian faith is not an idea, not an abstraction. It is personal commitment to God, the Creator, through one's own belief in the revelation manifest in the life and teaching of Jesus Christ. It is not to be judged by the canons of reason, nor to be tested by the perspectives of post-Enlightenment rationalism. Faith can never be proved or disproved by archaeologists.

Ironically, the study of archaeology helps clarify the contours and essence of faith. As G. Ernest Wright stated, "If there is a creative providence of God in history, it can only be observed in faith."[35] If the nineteenth century awakened us to Darwin's theory of evolution, twentieth-century archaeology has shown us that the most advanced cultures often are followed by inferior ones. Archaeological work can elicit reflections on the meaninglessness and chaotic dimensions of history. All, atheists and Christians alike, must admit that faith is not to be excavated from an archaeologist's balk or trench. It derives only from the perspective of the observer.

Christian faith does not peer dimly into the future and the past with little interest. It is not disoriented; it does not merely affirm general philosophical truths. It is focused on the particularities of a unique life lived out in one place and time. Since that life is none other than Jesus of Nazareth, and that place and time is Palestine before the burning of the Temple by the Roman soldiers in 70 C.E., it is imperative to know as much as possible about that life, that place, and that time.

Archaeology can help Christians comprehend their faith as they confess the Lordship of Jesus.[36] Those who have been with me in Israel on a personal pilgrimage or in an international seminar have shared such thoughts with me. In Galilee, I was privy to these words: "Now I more fully understand my faith, standing here east of the Sea of Galilee, in the ruins of Hippus, looking westward as the sun sets behind Mt. Tabor." In Jerusalem, at the spot where Jesus was probably crucified, I thought I heard these thoughts: "Jerusalem is real and not an ideal; Golgotha is not a part of a creed but an outcropping of white stone on which my Lord was crucified." These Christians were certainly not converted by archaeology, but after seeing and studying the origins of their faith they were changed; their faith clarified and amplified.

Barth was on the right track when he stressed that Paul's message fortunately is for all Christians today and not just for those dedicated to the kingdom of God in the first century. We are also heading in the right direction by stressing that archaeology is an antidote for the heresy that has plagued Christology and Christian faith from the end of the first to the end of the twentieth centuries. Jesus was not a being of celestial substance. He did not only appear to be a human being. He was, as the creeds remind us, "fully human."[37]

Now, thanks to archaeology, we can hold a coin similar to the one Jesus used when he said, "Render unto Caesar the things that are Caesar's and to God the things that are God's." And the face on the coin in our hands is that of Caesar, a man now dead and gone.

We can also now hold in our hands a Herodian lamp and comprehend more deeply Jesus' story of the foolish virgins who did not bring enough oil to refill their tiny lamps. Moreover, through various other additional archaeological finds from first-century Palestinian Jews, we can begin to imagine what the man Jesus must have been like. Then we are freed from the perennial temptation to make him a model man in our own image. Most excitingly, we are freed from the cancer of Docetism and the false belief that Jesus only appeared to be human. If that is the only service archaeology can help render to faith, it will have been one that saves the body of the faith. In brief, archaeology cannot form faith, but it can help inform faith.[38]

Notes

1. For a photograph, see J. Finegan, *The Life of Jesus and the Beginning of the Early Church* (Princeton: Princeton University Press, 1969), 249.

2. As quoted by R. de Vaux, "On Right and Wrong Uses of Archaeology," in *Near Eastern Archaeology in the Twentieth Century: Essays in*

Honor of Nelson Glueck, ed. J. A. Sanders (Garden City, N.Y.: Doubleday, 1970), 67. G. Garner rightly warns about the misuse of archaeology for apologetics. See his "Archaeology as a Tool: The Role of Archaeology in Relation to the Bible," *Buried History* 22 (1986): 75-93. One can appreciate William Dever's avoidance of the term "biblical archaeology" because it conjures up the mistaken notion that a scholar intends to "prove" the Bible "true," but at the same time there is much wisdom in H. Darrell Lance's claim that the substituted term "Syro-Palestinian archaeology" fails to represent the wide geographical range of biblical archaeological research. See P. J. King, *American Archaeology in the Mideast: A History of the American Schools of Oriental Research* (Philadelphia: ASOR, 1983), 270-72.

3. W. Keller, *The Bible as History: Archaeology Confirms the Book of Books*, trans. W. Neil (London: Hodder & Stoughton, 1956).

4. Plato, Hippias major 285d.

5. See de Vaux, "Right and Wrong Uses of Archaeology," 64-80.

6. Hence it also involves palaeography and encompasses philology.

7. R. de Vaux, "Right and Wrong Uses of Archaeology," 65.

8. K. M. Kenyon, *The Bible and Recent Archaeology*, rev. P. R. S. Moorey (Atlanta: John Knox Press, 1987), 11.

9. J. H. Charlesworth, *Jesus Within Judaism: New Light from Exciting Archaeological Discoveries*, Anchor Bible Reference Library 1 (New York: Doubleday, 1988), 109-15.

10. Ibid., 123-30.

11. For a photograph, see ibid., illustration 10; a more magnified view is presented in J. H. Charlesworth, ed., *Jesus' Jewishness: Exploring the Place of Jesus in Early Judaism* (New York: The American Interfaith Institute and Crossroad, 1991), illustration.

12. For a photograph of the Herodium, see Charlesworth, *Jesus Within Judaism*, illustration 7; for an artist's rendering of Masada, see idem, illustration 9.

13. I. Carmi concluded that "the boat began its life as a fishing vessel on the Sea of Galilee in 40 B.C." (p. 30). See his comments in S. Wachsam, "The Galilee Boat: 2,000-Year-Old Hull Recovered Intact," *Biblical Archaeology Review* 14 (1988): 19-33.

14. For photographs of the house, see Charlesworth, *Jesus Within Judaism*, illustrations 11 and 12.

15. It is conceivable, but unlikely, that the fire is the result of the prior internecine struggle among the Jews.

16. 11QTemple 50.10-19, "And if a woman is pregnant and her child dies in her womb, all the days that it is dead within her she is as unclean as a grave. Every house that she enters shall be unclean, and all its vessels... and all clay vessels shall be smashed, for they are unclean and will not become clean again."

17. A synchronism results from mentioning more than one chronological reference; see Luke 3:1.

18. For photographs and discussion, see G. Barkay, *Ketef Hinnom: A Treasure Facing Jerusalem's Walls* (Jerusalem: The Israel Museum, 1986), 29-31, 35-36.

19. For photographs and a discussion, see N. Avigad, "The Inscribed Pomegranate from the 'House of the Lord'," *Biblical Archaeologist* 53 (1990): 157-66.

20. See D. Syon, "Gamla: Portrait of a Rebellion," *Biblical Archaeology Review* 18 (1992): 21-37, 72.

21. See E. M. Meyers, E. Netzer, C. L. Meyers, "Sepphoris—Ornament of all Galilee," *Biblical Archaeologist* 49 (1986): 4-19.

22. See N. Avigad, *Discovering Jerusalem* (Nashville:Thomas Nelson, 1983).

23. The translation of J. Christiaan Beker, published in his *Paul the Apostle: The Triumph of God in Life and Thought* (Philadelphia: Fortress Press, 1980), 65.

24. I am indebted at this point to discussions with Professor D. Migliore.

25. See the caveats and insights written by de Vaux, "Right and Wrong Uses of Archaeology," 69, 78. R. de Vaux, one of my former teachers, was correct in almost everything he states in this article, but many of the English words attributed to him tend to misrepresent his major point, that is, to use archaeology to verify or to establish facts would be "a tendentious use of archaeological facts" (p. 78).

26. A. Schweitzer, *The Quest of the Historical Jesus: A Critical Study of Its Progress from Reimarus to Wrede*, trans. W. Montgomery (London: A.& C. Black, 1910).

27. Charlesworth, *Jesus Within Judaism*. See the comments by H. Anderson, *Jesus* (Englewood Cliffs, N.J.: Prentice-Hall, 1967), 24.

28. S. G. F. Brandon, *Jesus and the Zealots* (New York: Charles Scribner's Sons, 1968).

29. A. B. Cleage, Jr., *The Black Messiah* (New York: Sheed and Ward, 1968).

30. H. St. Chamberlain, *Foundations of the Nineteenth Century*, 2 vols., trans. John Lees (New York: John Lane Co., 1910).

31. J. Middleton Murry, *The Life of Jesus* (London: Jonathan Cape, 1926).

32. Lord Beaverbrook, *The Divine Propagandist* (London: Heinemann, 1962).

33. W. E. Phipps, *Was Jesus Married?* (New York: Harper & Row, 1970).

34. J. Schaberg, *The Illegitimacy of Jesus* (New York: Harper & Row, 1987).

35. G. E. Wright, *The Old Testament and Theology* (New York: Harper & Row, 1969), 85. I. T. Ramsey rightly stresses that although we Christians "cannot be content merely with historical facts," we cannot conclude that faith "might just as well be based on none at all, or that no 'facts' matter" (p. 216). Ramsey, "History and the Gospels: Some Philosophical Reflections," *Texte und Untersuchungen* 88 (1964): 201-17.

36. See the related comments on Bultmann and archaeology by G. E. Wright in *The Old Testament and Christian Faith: A Theological Discussion*, ed. B. W. Anderson (New York: Harper & Row, 1963), 180-81.

37. See 2 John, vs. 7.

38. Obviously, the question of the relation of archaeology to faith is related to but not identical with the perennial question of the relation of history (and historical knowledge) to faith. See the recent reflections by A. N. Wilder titled, "Norman Perrin and the Relation of Historical Knowledge to Faith," *Harvard Theological Review* 82 (1989): 201-11. I am convinced that Perrin's second and third levels of knowledge of Jesus Christ—"historic" knowledge and "faith" knowledge because of kerygmatic affirmation of Jesus as Lord—are impossible without the first level, specifically "historical" knowledge of Jesus that is documentable. This first level intersects with archaeology. Although Wilder does not mention archaeology, he does open a new and more sensitive approach to Christian origins by asking us to be less critical and more appreciative of the dynamic world of experience in which kerygmata appeared.

Chapter 2

Some Implications of Archaeology for New Testament Studies[1]

James F. Strange

What can archaeology do and not do for biblical studies?[2] Although this question has been asked many times, it seems that a problem lurks within the glib answers we often provide. Stated simply, the problem is that it is not actually clear what archaeology can do for biblical studies. This is particularly true in this century when biblical studies in general and New Testament studies in particular have drifted into a thoroughly theological mode in which the questions that archaeologists ask are in no wise those of the New Testament scholar. Perhaps one example can suffice. Typically, the archaeologist will contend that he or she is "digging up history," which is often taken to mean that archaeology is the handmaid of history. This is certainly true of the use to which scholars in other disciplines put archaeological discoveries. There is a long and honorable history of using archaeological "facts" to write economic histories, histories of art and architecture, and even the history of religions.[3] It is simply unthinkable to write a modern

history of Rome, Athens, or any other major city, such as
Jerusalem, without a thorough control of the archaeological
evidence. Yet the "facts" that the archaeologist adduces often
seem debatable, or subject to another interpretation that
places the find outside the limits of the time span in which
the New Testament was written, or simply of no direct
relevance to the historian and New Testament scholar. For
example, certain scholars have inquired whether they should
bother to read reports on the recent archaeology of
Jerusalem, since nothing so far found settles the question of
the location of Golgotha or the Praetorium, or they are not
intersted in pottery, or they cannot understand how questions of the "Third Wall" of Jerusalem impinge on study of
the New Testament text.

Lee I. Levine, a distinguished Israeli scholar, has recently
offered a response to the question of the relation of literary
to archaeological evidence. Levine asserts that there are three
ways of looking at that relationship: (1) "Sometimes archaeological material will confirm extant literary data to a
remarkable degree, as was the case with Masada." (2) "In
other instances, archaeology will supplement and complement literary data, adding new and important dimensions to
our understanding of the past. Urban discoveries are mostly
of this order." (3) "In certain cases, archaeological material
has raised new questions and issues, at times even
revolutionizing our understanding of the past . . . examples
are Qumran and, to a lesser extent, Beth She'arim."[4]

Although Levine does not mention the New Testament,
it would be part of what he calls "the quantity of literary
material available from this period." Levine's three
categories, therefore, surely pertain. However, it seems clear
that there is a missing element in his analysis. Precisely *how*
does archaeological material confirm literary data? Surely
the answer is in the missing middle term or middle stage. A
model of the social world of an ancient society derived from
archaeological material can confirm or contradict, i.e., *test* a
model of the social world of an ancient society derived from

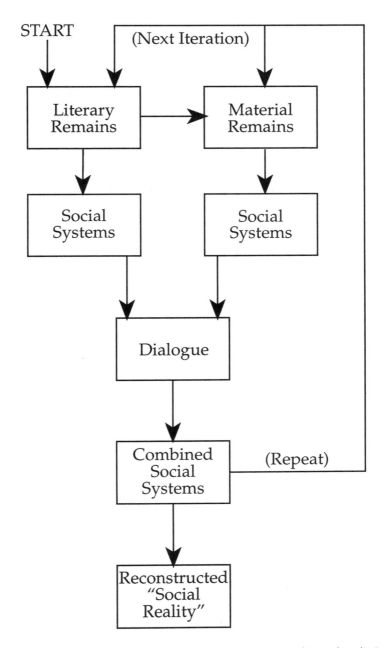

Figure 1. Block Diagram of the Dialogical Process of Reconstruction of "Social Reality" from Material and Literary Remains.

the literature. Archaeological materials cannot confirm or deny New Testament studies directly. In reality, only when two thought worlds collide do new ideas emerge. In the present instance, the reference is specifically to the contrast of a reconstruction drawn from the New Testament with a reconstruction drawn from the archaeological evidence[5] (see Fig. 1).

The roots of this idea go back to the twenties of this century. At that time, a flurry of scholarship emerged that was concerned with the social teachings and social origins of the New Testament. Shirley Jackson Case had helped set the stage in 1914 with *The Evolution of Early Christianity*. But it was his work entitled *The Social Origins of Christianity*, published in 1923, that entered the mainstream of New Testament scholarship precisely at the time when American Christian social concern was at its height.[6] Other scholars participated in this surge of interest in the social framework of the gospels and other writings of the New Testament, such as Frederick Grant, *The Economic Background of the Gospels*, first published in 1926.[7] Case scored again in 1934 with the publication of *The Social Triumph of the Ancient Church*,[8] though a backlash was now evident in American Christianity, moving from social concerns to more dogmatic ecclesiastical and theological concerns characteristic of the 1930s. Case, then, not only rode a wave, but helped create it with his own understanding of the social nature of early Christianity.

Perhaps one of Case's more interesting contributions, in retrospect, was his insistence on the urban character of life in ancient Palestine, including Galilee, and on the urban influence on Jesus. For example, in a brief article in 1926, Case argued that the proximity of Nazareth to Sepphoris and Yapha suggested that Nazareth was hardly secluded, as Klausner had proposed. Rather, it is possible, Case wrote, that Jesus made important social contacts during his youth and early manhood at Sepphoris and Yapha.[9] Case drew a picture in which Sepphoris was a political and commercial center second only to Jerusalem, and Nazareth was virtually a suburb of the largest city in Galilee. As a consequence, Jesus was heavily influenced by Sepphoris, particularly since Jesus may well have worked at Sepphoris as a carpenter or as a worker in the building trade in general. But Case wished to make the point that the urban center of Sepphoris would have offered opportunity for Jesus to encounter people of differing class and background. These encounters produced an unconventional Jesus who mixed freely with common people, who was generous to the stranger and outcast, and who was convinced of the equality of the classes before God. Furthermore, Case argued that in Jesus' view, which was not a village view, religion was part of one's daily life, not something that required withdrawal, as in the case of John the Baptist.[10]

Although certain reviewers of Case's *Jesus, a New Biography* (1927), such as Henry J. Cadbury of Bryn Mawr College, heartily approved of this emphasis,[11] continued stress on an urban element in the Jesus story virtually disappeared from biographies of Jesus written after this date. Thus one of Case's most interesting and original contributions did not take root in American, British, or continental New Testament scholarship.[12]

Modern sociological studies of the New Testament manage to ask questions of urbanization usually as part of the analysis of the extent of Hellenization, and particularly in discussions of the urban ambience of Galilee. The usual operative assumption is that Hellenization was part of urbanization.[13] Thus Malina can distinguish villagers from the "urban elite" of the cities of Galilee and Judea.[14] Freyne, on the other hand, can detect four layers of Galilean society, the first of which are the peasants, and the last of which are the Jewish aristocracy of the cities.[15] Freyne has also affirmed that Klausner's thesis of the relative isolation of Nazareth is true of all the localities of Galilee. He has even gone so far as to say that the "sense of permanence" of the citizens of the interior of Galilee isolated them and rendered them relatively immune from the influence of urban centers, such as Sepphoris.[16] In other words, Galilee was especially suited to a rural or peasant style of life. Recently Freyne has again affirmed the essentially rural character of the Galilee, "though surrounded by a circle of Greek-style cities on the periphery."[17] These "Greek-style cities" appear to be Gadara, Tyre and Sidon, Caesarea Philippi, and the Decapolis (p. 143). Freyne adds that there are other cities "in the neighborhood of Galilee in the first century," namely, Ptolemais/Acco, Gaba and Scythopolis, Qedesh (sic), and Bethsaida-Julias.[18]

But clearly Sepphoris could not function as a part of this circle, since it stood on a hill virtually in the geographic center of lower Galilee, i.e., it was not confined to a periphery. Furthermore, it was the capital and foremost city of Galilee as early as Gabinius 57-55 B.C.E. (*Ant.* XV.5.4-91; *War* I.8.5-170.)[19]

Modern studies in the social setting of the New Testament, then, particularly of life in Galilee, inquire after (1) social organization and interaction, (2) political structures and governance, (3) institutions of worship, (4) economic questions, and (5) the ancient awareness of these dimensions of life among the citizens of Galilee, Jew and gentile.[20] But it seems that, as we pursue this line of questioning, it is imperative to come to terms with the powerful presence of Herod Antipas's first effort at city building—Sepphoris—in the center of lower Galilee. Furthermore, without archaeological evidence factored into these reconstructions, this inquiry would be based largely upon partial evidence, that of literature and perhaps epigraphy. Even if the latest manuscript discoveries were included, such an inquiry would be severely truncated.

There seems to be an interdependent relationship between inferences from the evidence of archaeology and inferences from the evidence of literature. Constant, close attention to both is required of the scholar who wishes to reconstruct the social environment that generated the gospels and perhaps other early Christian literature. There-fore, drawing upon a page from John Stambaugh, "art and literature provide evidence for the environment, the environ-ment makes the art and literature comprehensible in new ways."[21] In short, archaeology provides evidence for the social world of the time. On the other hand, that reconstructed social world forces us to view the literature in new and unexpected ways.

But archaeology makes its main contribution to under-standing or illuminating Christian and Jewish literature of the Roman period not by simply unearthing remains of buildings, streets, houses, and artifacts mentioned in those texts. Rather, archaeology enables the researcher (1) to dis-cern *patterns of evidence* and (2) to infer social descriptions of the people of ancient Galilee. Archaeology does so by under-standing monuments as part of the perceptual world or perceptual matrix of an ancient people, as part of their cog-nitive map, as it were. Therefore not only words but even pots themselves fit precisely into their ancient symbolic en-vironment. Material culture is a product of the conceptual and symbolic world from which it springs.

On the other hand, archaeology tests the theories of sociological structure derived from literary, epigraphic, or even coin evidence. Those reconstructions of social reality of Galilee based upon archaeology are to be tested against those derived from ancient literature and epigraphy, so that the two reconstructions can gradually come to correct and inter-penetrate one other and to approximate the clearest state of affairs. I call this a "dialogical method," and in the present instance we have a chance to indulge ourselves with one example, namely, the archaeology of Sepphoris and parallel sites. After all, in the archaeology of the villages of Galilee and in the archaeology of Sepphoris, Tiberias, Acco-Ptolemais, Beth Shean, and Magdala we have an excellent source for understanding the social context of the Galilean ministry of Jesus and the emergence of the gospels.

In addition, we must expand the kinds of questions we ask of the material culture. Such an interpretive inquiry strains an archaeology with a poorly developed theoretical base. As long as we practice an archaeology with a poorly understood theory, we are in no better position than the historical scholar who knows nothing of historiography or critical methods in dealing with ancient texts.

We return to our original question: What is it that archaeology can do for New Testament studies? Archaeology can aid in establishing the social context in which the New Testament reports that the ministry of Jesus took place. This context includes details of economics, village/city relationships, the organization of Roman taxation, the extent of gentile and Jewish settlement in Galilee, resources for gentile worship, resources for Jewish worship, educational programs, and many other social systems.

Unfortunately, the process of archaeological inference is slow, for it relies upon deduction from the patterns of thousands of items in the archaeological record. Archaeologists move freely from the scientific method to intuitive methods to the methods of the *Geisteswissenschaften*, to use Dilthey's term.[22] This is frustrating to the nonarchaeologist who wishes to see within some reasonable time a definitive statement about education and academies in Galilee or the extent of gentile presence (or Jewish presence), and so forth. Only in the last twenty years have archaeological methods grown sophisticated enough in data gathering, recording, and interpretation to allow us to begin to answer. Can anyone blame the New Testament scholars for withdrawing into theology?

In this connection, the intent of this chapter is to propose that archaeologists and New Testament scholars deal with the idea of urbanization in Galilee by appeal to recent studies of ancient Rome and certain provincial cities, such as Pompeii and Ostia. The few remaining pages will concentrate on the architectural context of Roman cities as a symbolic environment which both reflected and shaped political, administrative, commercial, domestic, religious, and social activities.[23]

Furthermore, this chapter advances the hypothesis that Galilee, specifically lower Galilee, offers as much urban as rural ambience to the Galileans. This is because (1) a great walled city of revered antiquity, yet of recent reconstruction, namely, Sepphoris, lay in the center of that region; (2) the Galileans received the services of the city directly from Sepphoris, Tiberias, and Magdala-Taricheae after 20 C.E.; and (3) urbanism, the general trend in the Middle East throughout human history, was especially evident from the time of Alexander the Great.[24]

Finally, if the context of earliest Christianity and of developing rabbinic Judaism was as much urban as it was rural, then it follows that the descriptors of the people in village settings *and* urban centers are the descriptors of the social world of early Christianity and formative Judaism.

URBANIZATION IN THE ROMAN PERIOD

To explore further the contribution of archaeology to New Testament studies, I want to elaborate an idea inspired by some of the current literature in urban studies in archaeology. The idea is that Rome imposed a distinctive *urban overlay* upon a base, namely, the local, Jewish culture in first-century B.C.E. Judea.[25] This idea, which seems to have some explanatory power when dealing with Roman and Jewish culture, is so simple that one may miss its ability to account for certain matters in understanding the coming—and staying—of ancient Rome to Judea, Samaria, and Galilee.

Rome imposed this urban overlay for the simple reason that Rome was an expanding urban civilization. It was not the case—and I have repeated the error myself—that Rome had a "policy of urbanization."[26] Rather, as Rome exercised her expansionist goals and actually annexed Judea, Roman culture advanced over the local Jewish culture rather like a warm weather front advances over the terrain. To put this in cultural terms, as the invaders arrived, Roman culture superimposed itself upon the existing Jewish and

Hellenized-Jewish culture as the Romans superimposed themselves onto local Jewish society. The Romans as conquerers occupied the top layer of the society, generally speaking. The two layers of culture (the Roman overlay, the Jewish foundation or base) each generated artifacts, architecture, *symbols* expressed as artifacts and architecture, and patterns of distribution characteristic of that layer.[27] It happens that architecture is the easiest archaeological find to describe and reconstruct on paper. But architecture bears its own symbolic burdens of power and authority, social role, status, social identity of a people, acceptable entertainment, and the like.[28] In other words, this "urban overlay," especially as it came to expression in artifacts and architecture, bore the major institutions, ideas, and symbols of Roman culture in Judea. The local Jewish culture, on the other hand, bore its own institutions, ideas, and symbols.[29]

To the degree that the dominant culture was similar to ideas, customs, and symbols in the local culture, the overlay could in effect be a successful graft onto the local culture (to use a different image). In the case of Rome and ancient Judea, the degree of Hellenization of local culture would probably work in favor of the assimilation of Roman culture in Judea. That is, Rome could simply co-opt existing Hellenistic structures and symbols in Judea and Galilee. On the other hand, the degree of "strangeness" of either culture, from the other's perspective, no doubt inhibited the success of this graft.[30] Thus Acco-Ptolemais was considered an unclean city within its city walls and was excluded from the land of Israel by the rabbis, probably because it was too successfully Roman.[31]

As a matter of fact, the Jewish culture was already rural and urban and to some extent Hellenized, and therefore prepared for Roman dominance. Eventually (precisely when is up for debate) the clear distinction between the Roman urban overlay and the local Jewish base disappeared. However, it seems apposite to emphasize that even when the line between the two was blurred or absent, uniquely Jewish institutions and symbols survived as Jewish culture, as their

Roman counterparts survived within distinctively Roman culture. In other words, the difference was one of the focus and the center of either culture, not of the boundary between the two.

Yet the boundary is a more or less symbolic neutral zone between the two cultures. This boundary is populated by forms and symbols that are so generalized in meaning and function within the culture that they are not to be identified with any one social group of the culture, and can be used by both.

To clarify further, the symbols of specifically Roman culture, sometimes on a co-opted Hellenistic base, include baths, hippodromes, theatres, amphitheaters or circuses, odeons, nymphaea, figured wall paintings, statues, triumphal monuments, temples (Augustaea, Tiberia), etc.[32] Stambaugh has pointed out that what imposes itself upon the Roman materials is (1) a Roman approach to space that includes subduing, enclosing, regularizing, and imposing human technology, *and* putting up a striking facade; and (2) the habit of the upper classes of using games and buildings to affirm their position at the top of the social hierarchy.[33] In the latter case, we need the architecture of games as well as of prestige monuments to fulfill that interest.

Symbols of the Jewish foundation include the Second Temple, synaogues or places of assembly, art forms with Jewish symbols (menorah, ethrog, lulab), and tombs. We do not yet know the distinctive Jewish features that impose themselves upon the Jewish materials in the same sense as we understand the Roman ones.

Symbols of the interface between the two cultures in Galilee include basilicas, markets, agoras, colonnaded streets, ordinary houses, city walls, common pottery, and coinage, even though coins also provide space for Roman propaganda and other Roman ideas.

A second clarification, however, is in order. Since the idea of "urbanism" builds upon the idea of a city, it is important to explain what is meant by the term "city." Here the interest is not so much in the classical, political definitions of the *polis*,[34] nor in anthropological definitions that measure the number of types of institution represented at a given locality in order to arrive at a quantitative definition of the term.[35] Rather, in the tradition of the social archaeologists and social historians (and, perhaps, Wilhelm Dilthey), we can think of a city as a model or a conceptual prototype in the mind of a people.[36] As a part of people's background knowledge, the city is a conceptual artifact of the culture. That is, the idea "city" in ancient Judea expressed what the locals had in mind, no more and no less. It is not basically a foreign idea with which they found themselves burdened.[37]

It follows, then, that the citizens of the city, as they lived their lives in any given environment, gave expression to their idea of a city by planning the city, building it, and living in it. This activity left an imprint of the collective idea in the environment and in the material culture. This imprint is the city as artifact, reflecting the degree to which the city belongs to the urban overlay and the degree to which it belongs to the Jewish foundation or base. It is also this imprint to which the archaeologist as archaeologist gives attention. The archaeologist may also attempt to *infer* the city as idea, but at that point he or she is no longer simply an archaeologist and has become a social anthropologist or a social historian as well.[38]

Anthropologists have shown us that human beings almost everywhere on the planet develop urban civilizations. It is no accident that Rome was an urban civilization. That was not always so, but in the course of the development of Rome as a civilization, the city became simultaneously a major idea and a major artifact of that civilization. To put it another way, as Rome became expansionist and developed an empire, Rome and its clients did so most naturally (apart from military conquest) through the founding of cities and the redefining as Roman of certain non-Roman cities already in existence. Thus the Herods built Caesarea and Tiberias from the ground up as Roman cities. On the other hand,

Herod the Great redefined Jerusalem by renovation and reconstruction as a Roman city. Likewise, Samaria had already existed as an Israelite city, so Herod both rebuilt it and renamed it Sebast), a new Roman city, thereby redefining and claiming it as a part of the urban overlay.[39] In the second century, the Romans would redefine Jerusalem by destruction, refounding, rebuilding, and renaming.

In a similar vein, Sepphoris had already existed from antiquity, but Herod Antipas rebuilt it from its ruins after its destruction by Varus, the Syrian governor. This rebuilding was his opportunity to redefine Sepphoris as a Roman city for his patrons, the Romans, and thereby absorb Sepphoris into the Roman urban overlay.[40] In other words, now Antipas had the chance to achieve a classic Roman synthesis of foreign innovation and local tradition. The current excavations at Sepphoris, therefore, afford the scholarly world an excellent test case—though not the only one—for distinguishing local institutions and symbols and their Roman counterparts in the archaeological record.

So what are some of the elements of the Roman overlay in Palestine that we can identify, and what is their relationship to local Jewish traditions? One of the first that we can name is Roman administration, and this means most pointedly the governor at Caesarea and his bureaucracy.

Lee Levine has stressed that the choice of Caesarea as the seat of the new provincial government had symbolic power for Rome.[41] In effect Rome, through Herod the Great, served notice that Jerusalem was no longer the center as it had been, that new rulers required new administrative forms, and that these new forms were best located in a new administrative center.

But new forms and new institutions require new architecture. So the Roman overlay, now imposed on the old Hellenistic village of Strato's Tower, both established new administrative institutions and built new buildings. Thus Caesarea was graced with tax offices, courts, a consilium, "civic halls" (*Ant.* XV.9.6, par. 331), a mint, likely a forum and basilica, and other administrative offices.[42] A similar list could be developed for any major city in ancient Judea that functioned as an administrative center for the Romans, such as Sepphoris.[43]

One of the most distinctive ideas of Greco-Roman culture is of education in rhetoric rather than merely in philosophy. The institution that taught rhetoric was the gymnasium. Therefore, when the authors of Maccabees wished to charge the Jerusalemites with extremism in the adoption of Hellenism, they indicted them for building a gymnasium (1 Macc. 1:14; 2 Macc. 4:9, 12). But we know of archaeological remains of gymnasia at Kanawat in Syria, Gerasa, Philadelphia, Petra, Tyre, Sidon, Damascus, Ptolemais, Scythopolis, and Jericho, in addition to Jerusalem.[44]

James Kinneavy has shown us that the other Greco-Roman educational institution we should expect to find in a city of the eastern Roman empire is that of the *ephbia*, but as yet we have no evidence for these.[45]

THE SYMBOLIC POWER OF
ROMAN CITY PLANNING AND ARCHITECTURE

In the case of city planning, although the Roman city plans were not hippodamian at first, they certainly became so by the first century C.E.[46] Thus the new, regular grid for Jerusalem, posited by Wilkinson, would powerfully bespeak the transforming presence of Rome.[47] But the same respect for a geometric grid can be detected by archaeological means at Antipatris, Caesarea, Sepphoris, Scythopolis, Capernaum, Magdala, Sebast), Petra, Gerasa, and probably Herodian Jericho and Greater Herodium. In other words, at these sites one can lay eyes upon the imprint of the Roman idea of the city. One could walk through the artifact of the idea. One could directly and nonverbally experience the presence of Rome—the urban overlay as an expression of the specifically Roman aesthetic sense, Roman orderliness and symmetry.

Certain architectural forms not only function as symbols of the presence of Rome but also for certain Roman ideas, especially the Roman passion for entertainment, as represented by the erection of theaters, amphitheaters, stadiums, and hippodromes.[48] Theaters are now well-attested from archaeological remains at Bosra, Kanawat, el-Hammeh, Gerasa, Philadelphia, Philipopolis, Jericho (a theater/hippodrome), Petra, Caesarea, Sepphoris, Halutsa, Sebast), Neapolis, Scythopolis, and perhaps Legio.[49] A theater at Jerusalem is known from Josephus (*Ant.* XVII.10.2-255).

My purpose, however, is not simply to list these remains. It does not matter whether anyone launches a production in the theater building—although I would find an unused theater to be an improbable state of affairs—for the theater itself announces "Rome!" as clearly as a Latin augur announces Roman signs. The theater belongs to the Roman urban overlay and to the earlier Hellenistic and urban overlay. To illustrate, when the young sons of Herod were in Rome receiving their Roman education or acculturation, they could see and attend at least three theaters. The stone theater of Pompey was finished in 55 B.C.E., complete with a temple to Venus Vecatrix at the top row of seats. Lucretius speaks of the theaters and amphitheaters as the landmarks of the city. This theater was repaired by Augustus, and in 13 B.C.E., his small Theatrum Balbi was dedicated. A few years later the imposing Theater of Marcellus was dedicated in the Forum Holitorium.[50] It is interesting to note that there was a proliferation of theaters in the Augustan period, including the Theater at Orange of the first century B.C.E.,[51] the theater of Agrippa at Ostia,[52] and two theaters at Pompeii. The theater of Maius at Pompeii is usually assigned to this period.[53] In addition the Theatrum Tectum at Pompeii was built about 80 B.C.E., but was also refurbished in the Augustan period.[54]

The hippodrome is also a uniquely Roman institution, as well as a cultural artifact of the Roman thrill at the race. The hippodrome is well known at Caesarea and Jerusalem, though less well known are hippodromes at Taricheae (*War* 2.599, 606), Sebasté, Greater Herodium(?), Jericho, Gerasa, and other eastern Mediterranean cities.[55]

It seems clear that a pagan temple functions as a symbol par excellence for the presence, power, and dominance of Rome in a province. The appearance of temples on Roman coinage does not argue for actual temples in every regional city, but does attest to the deliberate invoking of the symbolic presence of Rome.[56] It is easy to insist that Herod built temples to Augustus in order to cement political relations between his client kingdom and the mighty empire; it is also possible to argue that he had no real choice. As a client king, he would indeed erect, maintain, and embellish symbols of Roman power, even symbols that might potentially alienate him from the heart of the subordinate culture, Judaism. In so doing, he was serving the interests of the Roman empire and his own interest in survival.

But what was the relation of the ideas, institutions, and symbols in the overlay to distinctive Jewish institutions, culture, and ideas? Was the Jewish foundation in eternal conflict with the Roman urban culture imposed upon it? Surely the answer varies with whichever element of the culture is under discussion.

Martin Goodman has furnished a valuable analysis of the social conflict within Judea that made a devastating loss to Rome inevitable from 66-70 C.E. The Jewish upper classes themselves, the very ones that Rome would otherwise depend upon for controlling the masses of people in Judea, were not unified, nor were they in a position of power such as the Romans needed. It did not even matter that an external menace, Rome itself, was threatening the very existence of Jews and Judaism and the Jewish nation.[57] In other words, the power to annihilate, represented by Rome, could not insure a unified resistance from the Jews. Thus the urban overlay under discussion in no way simply controlled the ethnic unit that Judaism is sometimes understood to be. The

Roman urban overlay could not bring about political unity with the underlying Jewish culture.

In fact, as long as the functions of the institutions in the urban overlay and in the Jewish foundation were kept separate, Roman and Jewish institutions could thrive side by side. Therefore there was a well developed Roman court system in Caesarea and likely the regional capitals,[58] but there was also the parallel court system within Judaism.[59] For example, in ancient Judea, local judges and local courts settled disputes under one or more judges.[60] On the other hand, the Sanhedrin in Jerusalem operated much as a supreme court, even while the procurators heard their own Roman cases in Caesarea.[61]

We have already spoken of the gymnasia as eloquent tokens of the urban overlay imposed by Rome. Of course, the Jewish school system was in place in the first century C.E. and is well documented in Jewish sources.[62] There seems to be little overlap of gymnasia and Jewish school functions, suggesting that the Jewish school performed also as an operative symbol for Torah instruction and faithfulness to Torah within the Jewish community, just as study of rhetoric in the gymnasium did for Roman culture. The existence of the gymnasium in no way obviated the need for the Beth Midrash, since they functioned within two different worlds.

Jewish architecture seems to be difficult to pinpoint in the first century, even if it served well the needs of the Jewish foundation or base. The problem may be that architecture developed within the overwhelmingly powerful norms of Greek and Roman influence at first, which may make it all the more difficult to identify, even in the Second Temple. Nevertheless, one of the more intriguing aspects of those buildings tentatively identified as first century "synagogues" at Gamala, Capernaum, Magdala, and Masada is careful attention to simplicity and provision for mass seating.[63] Of course, absence of evidence proves nothing, but the striking absence of iconography alongside the Roman world, where iconography was everything, suggests the possibility of a non-Roman element. In this case, although the solution is controversial and likely unprovable, the iconographic silence of these buildings may enable them to speak all the more clearly for Judaism.

Earlier I mentioned that Sepphoris may afford the scholarly world an excellent test case for distinguishing local institutions and symbols and their Roman counterparts. Some data in support of this contention is already emerging. For example, both the University of South Florida Excavations at Sepphoris and the Joint Expedition to Sepphoris have uncovered otherwise ordinary Roman and Byzantine houses which happen to have *mikvaoth* or ritual baths beneath their floors.[64] These installations serve local Jewish custom, not the Roman presence. A famous Byzantine-era Greek inscription from Sepphoris mentions at least three generations of men with the title *archisynagogos*.[65] A certain Simon—a Jew—was city official for weights and measures, as his signed, standard weight was found. A spectacular find has been a dining room mosaic with scenes from the life of Dionysios.[66] Another find by the University of South Florida Excavations at Sepphoris has been a set of three bronze cultic objects that may indicate worship of Serapis at Sepphoris as late as the fourth century C.E. Jewish tombs from the site have been identified by their burial inscriptions, at least one of which featured a menorah.[67] Major public architecture, unearthed by the University of South Florida Excavations at Sepphoris, includes a bath or public ritual bath, a portion of an imposing Late Roman basilica or other collonaded building with at least two colored mosaic carpets, and a huge theater (first discovered in 1931 by Leroy Watermann of the University of Michigan) from the first century C.E.[68] We have also uncovered a major east-west street on the east side that may connect with the road to Tiberias. This street began its life in the Early Roman period. It is flanked by square rooms with heavy valuted roofs in typical Roman style at the south end. A remnant of what appears to be a huge Herodian period pool reveals attention to public water works on a large scale.

In other words, the excavations are turning up evidence precisely for the symbols of Roman power and cult in terms of large buildings and mosaic art, and also for local Jewish practice in homes concerned with ritual cleanliness.

There is surely more to be learned, and the distribution of the data unearthed may indeed test the hypothesis of a Roman urban overlay imposed upon a Jewish foundation or base. So far it appears that the symbols of Rome penetrate downward all the way to the level of domestic life while the symbols of Judaism are to be found precisely at the level of domestic life. In other words, so far the hypothesis of the "urban overlay" tends to be confirmed.

There are several conclusions to be gleaned from this analysis of the situation in Rome eastward to Galilee. One implication of the idea of the urban overlay is that earliest Christianity originated in Galilee in the local Jewish culture, but it could not avoid the Roman overlay. The spread of Christianity depended upon the network afforded by the Roman overlay. In fact, Christianity also depended upon urban centers to generate its literature, for it was precisely the learned or literati of the urban centers who provided that service.[69]

URBAN FEATURES OF MARK AND Q (and M)

At this stage, my intent is to show that, given the foregoing analysis, certain features of Mark and Q (and other gospel texts) are visible that might otherwise escape notice. In other words, the archaeological understanding that Galilee has an urban element forces us to see the urban elements in the text. Many of the metaphors and settings of individual pericopes are urban in character. A few of these features have been noticed for years, while others have been observed more recently by Sean Freyne, D. W. Bösen, and Douglas Edwards, among others.[70] My purpose here is to stimulate discussion, not to offer solutions to old conundrums about the origins and purposes of the synoptic gospels or of Q.

First, if we are to take Capernaum seriously as Jesus' base of operations, then one must call attention to a simple fact about Jesus' selection of Capernaum as his headquarters (recorded in Mark 1:21, Matt. 4:13; Luke 4:31), namely, that Jesus selected a town or large village that is a customs seat (Matt. 9:9) at the border with the city territory of Bethsaida-Julias.[71] This places the focus of his ministry on the main road that came inland at the Megiddo pass, turned north at Philoteria at the south end of the lake, followed a northward track around the west end of the lake through Tiberias, and continued north to Damascus at Heptapegon (modern Tabgha or Seven Springs) before Capernaum. An important leg of this road forked east through Capernaum to Bethsaida-Julias and points eastward.[72]

The geographical and political setting for this narrative and that of the call of the disciples (the latter is recorded in Mark 1:16-20; Matt. 4:18-22) is the well-populated, metropolitan strip of land and the highway from Philoteria through Sinnabris, through Hammath-Tiberias, to Tiberias, Magdala-Tarichaeae, the plain of Gennosaur, the deserted part (Seven Springs), and Capernaum. This location implies traffic, commerce, and the flow of ideas and information, including gossip.[73]

In the Q passage on the law and the prophets (Matt. 5:17-20; Luke 16:16-17), Jesus discusses the law and his relationship to it. Here the reader should ask what might be meant when Jesus refers to those who relax the commandments and teach others so. Who might he have in view? The simplest answer is a teacher who teaches in his own *yeshivah* or academy. And what do we know of first century academies? Very little, it seems.[74] Adolf Büchler, among others, has mentioned second- and third-century Jewish texts in which the rabbis attack the faithless teachers and students of Sepphoris and Tiberias.[75] If we imagine an academy as the situation presupposed by the story, then we are more likely to opt for an urban setting than a village setting. The economy of the village is not likely to have been able to support a rabbi and his academy.

In the Q passage on murder and wrath (Matt. 5:21-26; Luke 12:57-59), Jesus counsels his audience to "make friends quickly with your accuser, while you are going to court, lest your accuser hand you over to the judge, and the judge to the guard, and you be put in prison" (Matt. 5:25). The story presupposes a court system with a judge where citizens can sue one another, as well as a court guard or constable and jail—all of which, as a system, are part of city, not of village life.[76]

The Q passage on love of one's enemies (Matt. 5:43-48; Luke 6:27-28), mentions tax collectors. As far as we know, these are Jews (since there is discussion in Jewish sources of what to do about them when they repent)[77] who work out of offices in cities, though in the case of Matthew (Levi), in a frontier town.[78] They also can roam the countryside to search travelers and their loaded beasts of burden.[79] The Roman tax system is under discussion here. It is part of the Roman overlay, but it also penetrates down into the local Jewish culture as well.

On the other hand Matt. 5:48 and elsewhere mentions gentiles (Lukan parallel "sinners"). Formerly, this was regarded as support for the notion that Galilee was properly called "Galilee of the gentiles." We are now in a position to understand where these gentiles came from. The main places where Jews had occasion to meet non-Jews were the cities of Sepphoris, Tiberias, and above all, Acco-Ptolemais (but also in Hammath, Magdala, and possibly Gennosaur). The second meeting place was on the roads to market towns such as Tiberias and Sepphoris, and in the city markets themselves.[80]

The Q passage on the centurion of Capernaum (Matt. 8:5-13; Luke 7:1-10) is quite instructive in this regard. That Q presents a centurion in Capernaum in his own house, that is, a resident, implies that a contingent of Roman soldiers were stationed there, as these would not be Jewish soldiers. Perhaps the Roman soldiers formed a police force for the border town to assist Levi, the tax collector, in his work. This situation provided opportunity for Jews to encounter gentiles, even Romans, certainly including their dependents.

One of Richard Batey's more controversial ideas has been that the meaning of the word "hypocrite" in the canonical gospels should be understood in its root (Greek) meaning of "actor." This hypothesis allows us to see allusions to Roman entertainment in the theater, especially since we have a theater at Sepphoris.[81]

In Matt. 6:1-18, mostly unique to Matthew, we have a set of Jesus' teachings regarding almsgiving, prayer, fasting, and forgiveness. In this case, vs. 2 is translated in the NRSV as follows: "So whenever you give alms, do not sound a trumpet before you, as the hypocrites do in the synagogues and in the streets."[82] Here it is helpful to understand "synagogues" in the broadest sense as "public assemblies." Furthermore, if we notice that *plateion* is the plural of *plateia* or a collonaded street (the rabbis knew the word *plty'* for the main street of Sepphoris: y. Ketub.I.10), then we also translate 6:2 and 6:5 as follows: "So whenever you give alms, do not sound a tantara before you, as the actors do in the [public] assemblies and in the [colonnaded] streets," and "And whenever you pray, do not be like the actors; for they love to stand and pray in [public] assemblies and on the corners of the [collonaded] streets, so that they may be seen by others."[83]

According to Matt. 6:7 (unique to Matthew), Jesus' audience might encounter pagans "babbling" and piling up phrase on phrase, hoping to be heard by their gods. Surely this is a hint of public worship, that is, a temple in a city. Since Herod built a temple to Augustus both at Sebast) and at Caesarea, it is not beyond thought that some of the residents of Galilee knew what public pagan pomp and worship was like. This could, of course, occur at Acco, but perhaps also in other cities of Galilee.[84]

Furthermore, Matt. 6:16-18 (unique to Matthew) has presented a picture of hypocrites who paint their faces when they fast. Commentators have simply ransacked Jewish tradition, looking for a precedent which was not to be found.[85] If, on the other hand, we allow the Greek word to mean "actor," then we discover we are most likely talking about mimes who paint their faces. After all, the mime's face amounts to a public declaration of who he is, and they are to be found in cities, namely, in public gatherings (*synagogais*), on street corners, and other wide places designed for assemblies, as in a gymnasium.[86]

The Q passage on the two ways (Matt. 7:13-14; Luke 13:23-24) mentions the "narrow gate," which is a city gate, or at least a gate in a walled town. Villages did not have "gates," as far as we know. Luke mentions Nain as having a gate, which may make it a walled town.[87]

The context of Matt. 10:17-19 (Matthew only) must be urban, for the warning to Jesus' disciples is that they will be handed over to the *synedria*, flogged in public assemblies or "synagogues," and delivered (for judgment) to governors and kings. All of these elements are characteristic of cities, not of villages. That they are handed over or arrested implies a police force of Roman or Jewish soldiers such as at Sepphoris or one of the larger cities.[88]

In the long Q pericope on Jesus' witness concerning John (Matt. 11:7-19; Luke 7:24-34) stands the tale of children sitting in the market places (Matt. 11:16-17; Luke 7:31-32, *en tois agorais*). In these market places, the children saw both wedding and funeral processions, and imitated them. The wider context in Q is the woes upon the cities that did not repent: Chorazin, Bethsaida, and Capernaum. It is not likely that village squares are in view here.[89] We know from ancient literary notices that both Tiberias and Sepphoris had two market places each.[90] We cannot therefore argue that this pericope presupposes Sepphoris or Tiberias, but we must at least be open to the idea that Q's audience might think of the big market places with their large numbers of visitors from neighboring villages, including their children.

In a mechanized civilization like ours, we tend to forget how much of a market day is devoted to marketing, and how much to news, entertainment, and visiting friends. The Romans themselves founded market towns or *emporia*, which functioned within the Roman culture much as they would in Jewish culture.[91]

Matt. 13:24-30, or the parable of the Weeds among the Wheat (unique to Matthew), seems to presuppose an absentee landlord who did not regularly see his fields.[92] The theme of the city dweller who lets out his fields to others is also well known in Roman civilization, as Stambaugh has pointed out. These were citizens who lived within the walls of Rome, but whose farms were tended by slaves.[93] In like fashion, the servants of the householder (*oikodespotes* = "director of a house or family") in Matt. 13:24-30 have to tell him of the weeds among his wheat.[94]

Note also Matt. 13:45-46, or the parable of the Pearl of Great Value (Thomas 76). The pearl is found by a merchant (*anthropos emporos*), who is in search of pearls, presumably not in small villages, but among the valuables of the rich or in the major markets where these things are sold. Upon finding this pearl, he capitalizes all his goods in order to buy it. The sources of capital are normally understood to reside in cities and in certain towns where bankers live, for that is what the merchant needs.[95]

Finally, note the Q parable of the Great Banquet (Matt. 22:1-14; Luke 14:15-24). In this case, part of what is important is omitted and part is expressed. What is left out is the place of this great banquet.[96] We know from many Roman literary sources of banquets held either in great villas or in public banquet halls or in a triclinium. A second-story triclinium is mentioned at Sepphoris (Lev. Rab. c.16.2), and the Joint Expedition to Sepphoris has uncovered, in a villa, a Middle Roman triclinium with a magnificent mosaic.[97]

In this case, Jesus' audience could assume either context. Either way we are probably in a city, because a rich man is giving the banquet, and the very language of his instructions to his servant indicates that this parable is set in a city.

The first set of instructions to his servant (Luke 14:21) is, "Go out [of this hall] to the *plateias kai rumas*," which are apparently frequented by the "poor, maimed, blind, and lame." *Plateias kai rumas* are contrasted with *hodous kai phragmous* (14:23, "paths and hedges"). But "paths and hedges" belong to the countryside. The NRSV translates the former as "streets and lanes," the latter as "roads and lanes." Since we see *plateia* conjoined with *rumas*, normally understood in the sense of "narrow street, lane, or alley,"[98] it is not difficult to conclude that we should translate the first phrase as "colonnaded streets and side streets" (of a city). That leaves us with "roads and lanes" (in the countryside) for the second.

Thus the first set of instructions presupposes that the servant will go out of the hall into the Cardo Maximus of the city with its side streets, while the second presupposes that he will go outside the city walls to recruit diners. Either way, the setting and images of the story are urban.

In summary, then, we can say that reading the gospels probably requires us to recognize the complexities of a setting that uses urban as well as rural metaphors. These urban metaphors and settings for individual pericopes characterize some of the earliest layers of the gospel traditions. We need not look always to a redactor's hand when we encounter urban elements in the literary tradition. Furthermore, at least one implication stands clear: it is no longer possible to affirm the extreme, that the earliest Christian movement originated in a simple rural atmosphere. In other words, we do not need a Paul to urbanize and universalize the Christian movement; it was at least partially so from the beginning.

CONCLUSIONS

This is not yet a place for firm conclusions, but for conclusions in an interim sense. I see a major task facing archaeologists and textual (that is, biblical) scholars. It is the task of (1) constructing social histories of Israel in its various periods from archaeology, on the one hand, and (2) from literature, on the other. Then (3) these two social constructions must be brought into dialogue with one another so that the inconsistencies and holes in one construction can be corrected by the other, and vice versa. This collusive dialogue has the chance of opening up the text for us in ways that were closed before, as we disclose its contexts in new ways. The dialogue may also open up the world of archaeology for us in new ways, as we view the ancient literary context with renewed seriousness.

Notes

1. Certain portions of this paper were read in another form under the title "Urban Studies, Earliest Christianity, and Sepphoris" at the Annual Meeting of the Society of Biblical Literature, Nov. 20, 1988. In its present, strongly revised incarnation, it was read for the "Bible, Archaeology, and Faith" symposium at Florida Southern College, Lakeland, Fla., March 29-30, 1990. This paper has benefitted from criticism of many friends, including James H. Charlesworth of Princeton Theological Seminary, J. Maxwell Miller of Candler School of Theology, Dennis E. Groh of Garrett-Evangelical Theological Seminary, Thomas R. W. Longstaff of Colby College, Douglas Edwards of the University of Puget Sound, and Leslie J. Hoppe of Catholic Theological Union. I am myself to be held responsible for its errors and inadequacies.

2. H. Darrell Lance, *The Old Testament and the Archaeologist* (Philadelphia: Fortress, 1981); Leslie J. Hoppe, *What are they saying about Biblical Archaeology?* (New York and Ramsey, N.J.: Paulist Press, 1984). The classic statement is still Roland de Vaux, "On Right and Wrong Uses of Archaeology," in *Near Eastern Archaeology in the Twentieth Century: Essays in Honor of Nelson Glueck*, ed. James A. Sanders (Garden City, N.Y.: Doubleday, 1970), 64-80.

3. For example, the position of one of Europe's most distinguished archaeologists is that the task of archaeology is simply to establish the historical "facts." See Paul Courbin, *What is Archaeology? An Essay on*

the Nature of Archaeological Research, trans. P. Bahn (Chicago: University of Chicago Press, 1988), 131.

4. Lee I. Levine, "Archaeological Discoveries from the Greco-Roman Era," in *Recent Archaeology in the Land of Israel*, ed. Benjamin Mazar and Hershel Shanks (Washington, D.C.: Biblical Archaeology Society; Jerusalem: Israel Exploration Society, 1984), 75-87, esp. 76.

5. This is close to Heinrich Schuetzinger's corporation model of the relationship between biblical studies and the archaeological evidence. See his article "'Dies ist der Ord, von dem geschrieben steht...,'" *Biblische Notizen* 47 (1989): 35-89. I thank Dr. Leslie Hoppe for calling my attention to this reference.

6. Shirley Jackson Case, *The Evolution of Early Christianity* (Chicago: University of Chicago Press, 1914); idem, *The Social Origins of Christianity* (Chicago: University of Chicago Press, 1923).

7. Frederick C. Grant, *The Economic Background of the Gospels* (London: Oxford University Press, 1926).

8. Shirley Jackson Case, *The Social Triumph of the Ancient Church* (New York and London: Harper & Bros., 1934).

9. Shirley Jackson Case, "Jesus and Sepphoris," *Journal of Biblical Literature* 45 (1926): 14-22, esp. 15. See Joseph Klausner, *Jesus of Nazareth: His Times, His Life, and His Teaching*, trans. H. Danby (New York: Macmillan, 1925), 236-38.

10. Case, "Jesus and Sepphoris," 19.

11. Henry J. Cadbury, "The Historic Jesus," *Journal of Religion* 8 (1928): 130-36.

12. Shirley Jackson Case, *Jesus, a New Biography* (Chicago: University of Chicago Press, 1927). For a recent return to this theme, see Thomas R. W. Longstaff, "Sepphoris and Nazareth," in *Christ and His Communities*, Festschrift for Reginald Fuller (Cincinnati: Forward Movement Publications, 1990). For a survey of Jesus research from 1980 to 1984, see James H. Charlesworth, *Jesus within Judaism: New Light from Exciting Archaeological Discoveries* (New York: Doubleday, 1988), 187-207.

13. Cf. John E. Stambaugh and David L. Balch, *The New Testament in Its Social Environment*, Library of Early Christianity, ed. Wayne A. Meeks (Philadelphia: Westminster, 1986), 88f. John Gager distinguished an "urban plebs" or "urban proletariat" (the term in his index) in ancient Rome in *Kingdom and Community: The Social World of Early Christianity* (Englewood Cliffs, N.J.: Prentice-Hall, 1975). Gerd Theissen can assert, strangely enough, that Jews generally stayed away from the city states, which he avers was also true of the "Jesus movement," *Sociology of Early Palestinian Christianity*, trans. John Bowden (Philadelphia: Fortress, 1977), 69. Therefore Theissen marvels that the early Christian assemblies borrowed the term *ekklesia* from the constitution of the city state to denote their assemblies. If we grant that postbiblical Judaism and earliest Christianity were as much a phenomenon of the city as of the countryside, there is nothing to be surprised about.

14. Bruce J. Malina, *The New Testament World: Insights from Cultural Anthropology* (Atlanta: John Knox, 1981).

15. Sean Freyne, *Galilee from Alexander the Great to Hadrian, 323* B.C.E. *to 135* C.E.: *A Study of Second Temple Judaism* (Wilmington, Del.: Michael Glazier; Notre Dame: University of Notre Dame Press, 1980), 194-200.

16. Ibid., 16.

17. Sean Freyne, *Galilee, Jesus, and the Gospels: Literary Approaches and Historical Investigations* (Philadelphia: Fortress, 1988), 145. An interesting alternative hypothesis is offered by Howard Clark Kee, *Community of the New Age: Studies in Mark's Gospel* (Philadelphia: Westminster, 1977), 103. Kee shows, with some success, that Mark's gospel is anticity. But Roman authors were consistently anticity, even though they wrote in the cities. Thus ideological tendencies need not correlate with provenance.

18. It seems that Geza Vermes might be cited in support of the rural nature of Galilee; see esp. *Jesus and the World of Judaism* (Philadelphia: Fortress, 1984), 28; 159, n.6. However, Vermes seems to be emphasizing that Jesus' ministry was confined to the countryside or to rural Galilee. The alleged isolation of Galilee has been firmly rejected by Eric M. Meyers, "The Cultural Setting of Galilee: The Case of Regionalism and Early Judaism," *Aufstieg und Niedergang der Römischen Welt* 2.19.1 (1979): 686-702. On Qedesh as Cadasa in the Roman period, see Michael Avi-Yonah, *The Holy Land from the Persian to the Arab Conquest (536 B.C. to A.D. 640): A Historical Geography* (Grand Rapids, Mich.: Baker, 1977), 130.

19. Stuart S. Miller, *Studies in the History and Traditions of Sepphoris*, Studies in Judaism in Late Antiquity 37 (Leiden: E. J. Brill, 1984), 2.

20. Stambaugh and Balch, *New Testament in Its Social Environment*, 92-94; Emil Schürer, *The History of the Jewish People in the Age of Jesus Christ (175 B.C. - A.D. 135)*, vol. 1, rev. G. Vermes, F. Millar, and M. Black (Edinburgh: T & T Clark, 1979), 85-183, for a survey of Greek cities in Palestine.

21. John E. Stambaugh, *The Ancient Roman City, Ancient Society and History* (Baltimore: Johns Hopkins University Press, 1988), xv. It will be clear in this paper how much I am indebted to Stambaugh.

22. Wilhelm Dilthey, "Die Auslegung oder Interpretation," 216-20 of Dilthey, *Der Aufbau der Geschichtlichen Welt in den Geisteswissenschaften, Gessamelte Schriften*, vol. 7 (Stuttgart: B. G. Teubner, 1965).

23. Stambaugh, *Ancient Roman City*, xvi.

24. George McLean Harper, Jr., "Village Administration in the Roman Province of Syria," *Yale Classical Studies* (1928): 105-68, esp. 107. "The tendency of history seems to be for men to aggregate themselves in ever larger units." On the question of urbanism in ancient Israel, see Frank S. Frick, *The City in Ancient Israel*, Society of Biblical Literature Dissertation Series 36 (Missoula: Scholars Press, 1977).

25. The term "urban overlay" is from the essay by James F. Strange, "Two Aspects of the Development of Universalism in Christianity: The

First to the Fourth Centuries," in *Religion and the Global Order*, ed. Roland Robertson and William R. Garrett (New York: Paragon House, 1991), 35-63. The idea has some similarity to Colin Renfrew's "urban imposition" in *Approaches to Social Archaeology* (Cambridge: Harvard University Press, 1984), 112.

26. The classic statement is still A. Jones, "Urbanization in Palestine," *Journal of Roman Studies* (1931): 78. See also Avi-Yonah, *The Holy Land*, 108-80.

27. It is also the case that each layer and the boundary between the layers produced its own literature. Thus Robbins has recently argued that the Gospel of Mark is a product of that interface, or what he calls an "intercultural" document. See Vernon K. Robbins, "Interpreting the Gospel of Mark as a Jewish Document in a Greco-Roman World," *Studies in Judaism: New Perspectives on Ancient Judaism*, Society and Literature in Analysis 5, ed. Paul Virgil McCracken Flesher (Lanham, Md.: University Press of America, 1990), 47-72. On Hellenistic urbanization in Judea before the coming of Rome, see Shimon Applebaum, *Judea in Hellenistic and Roman Times Historical and Archaeological Essays* (Leiden: E. J. Brill, 1989).

28. Symbols of "prestige urbanism," Stambaugh, *Ancient Roman City*, 29, would include any imposing structure. Augustus also faced buildings with marble that were otherwise made of volcanic tufa and travertine, or a few of solid marble (Temple of Apollo Palatinus, the Temple of Jupiter Tonans, and the Ara Pacis). "I found the city made of brick and left it made of marble," Suetonius, *Augustus*, in Stambaugh, *Ancient Roman City*, 51. In like manner, Sepphoris covered its buildings with up to nine different kinds of marble. We have found fragments of one green marble column, seventy-two centimeters in diameter. This is an attempt to make the urban environment conform to the appearance of the Roman overlay.

29. This position argues against E. Rivkin, "The Internal City: Judaism and Urbanization," *Journal for the Scientific Study of Religion* 5 (1965/66): 225-40. In spite of his otherwise useful insights, the introduction of Greek *polis* to the ancient Near East was probably not as disruptive as Rivkin believes. On the other hand, this essay is closer to the conceptual territory of Colin Renfrew in *Peer Polity Interaction and Socio-political Change*, ed. Colin Renfrew and John F. Cherry, New Directions in Archaeology Series (Cambridge: Cambridge University Press, 1986), esp. p. 2, where cities are called "early states" or "early state modules."

30. As has been argued for Roman Syria. See Peter Brown, "Town, Village, and Holy Man: The Case of Syria," in his *Society and the Holy in Late Antiquity* (Berkely: University of California Press, 1982), 153-65. On p. 163, n.25, Brown cites Palestine as an area of "mixed allegiance" in late antiquity. Perhaps Brown's idea of a "community of values" (163) is of importance in explaining the success of a Roman graft on the Jewish culture.

31. See M. Gittin 1:2C: "From Akko and northward, and Akko is equivalent to territory north of Akko," in Jacob Neusner, *The Mishnah: A New Translation* (New Haven: Yale University Press, 1988). The coins of Acco-Ptolemais are especially rich in pagan symbolism, including depictions of Aphrodite, Artemis, Heracles, Perseus and the Medusa, Roman standards, Serapis, Tyche, and Zeus. See Ya'akov Meshorer, *City-Coins of Eretz-Israel and the Decapolis in the Roman Period* (Jerusalem: The Israel Museum, 1985), 11-15.

32. The co-opting of Hellenistic forms in Galilee may be no more than an expression of the *mos maiorum* or "way our ancestors did things," to borrow an idea from Stambaugh, *Ancient Roman City*, 55. The combining of Hellenistic and Roman forms would be a classic Roman synthesis. It will be the task of archaeology to see if Roman architects of the Augustan age in Galilee synthesized Roman with Hellenistic elements or with neo-Attic Greek forms of the fifth century B.C.E.

33. Stambaugh, *Ancient Roman City*, xv.

34. For a useful discussion of the Greek *polis*, see Marcel Détienne, "Les chemins de la deviance: Orphisme, Dionysisme et Pythagorisme," in [*Atti del Quattordicesimo*] *Convengno di Studi sulla Magna Grecia: Orfismo in Magna Grecia* (Naples: Arte Tipographia, 1975), 49-78.

35. As in Moses Finley, *The Ancient Economy* (London: Chatto and Windus, 1973). I heartily concur with the position of Albrecht Alt who makes urbanism a power question, not a size question, in "Galiläische Probleme," *Kleine Schriften zur Geschichte der Volkes Israel*, vol. 2 (Münich: C. H. Beck'sche Verlag, 1953), 384ff.

36. Joseph Rykwert, *The Idea of a Town: The Anthropology of Urban Form in Rome, Italy, and the Ancient World* (Princeton: Princeton University Press, 1976), 25. See Dilthey, *Der Aufbau der Geschichtlichen Welt in den Geisteswissenschafter, Gessamelte Schriften*, vol. 7, 216-20. If we take this position, we must look for tangible expressions of that idea in the monuments of the city. For another approach based on internal organization, political independence, and diverse population, see Freyne, *Galilee, Jesus, and the Gospels*, 145-46. For an archaeological perspective that I find congenial and herein assume, see Colin Renfrew, *Towards an Archaeology of Mind: An Inaugural Lecture Delivered before the University of Cambridge on 30 November 1982* (Cambridge: Cambridge University Press, 1982).

37. In his criticism of this chapter, Max Miller has suggested that we translate "urban/rural" into modern terms that are closer to the ancient reality. He has suggested "town/village," which seems apposite. The reader is warned that the split between city and countryside is nowhere near as dramatic a split as we experience today. Early Roman Jerusalem was little more than one square mile in area, which is next to nothing by modern standards. That a "walled city" need not be of any size is clear from the legal discussion in M. Arak. 9:6 "A: [A house

in a city] roofs of which form its wall; B: or one in a city which was not surrounded by a wall from the time of Joshua ben Nun; C: is not deemed *a dwelling house in a walled city*. D: [And what is *a dwelling house in a walled city*?] E: [A house in which are not less than] three court-yards, each with two houses, surrounded by a wall since the time of Joshua ben Nun, such as the old castle of Sepphoris, the fortress of Gush Halab, old Yodpat, Gamala, Gadwad, Hadid, Ono, Jerusalem, and the like," in Neusner, *Mishnah*, 823.

38. This is the position of Courbin, *What is Archaeology*, 122-24, and ad loc., but Courbin rejects the role of historian for the archaeologist. I am willing to affirm it.

39. On the Herods as city founders and rebuilders, see Harold W. Hoehner, *Herod Antipas: A Contemporary of Jesus Christ*, new ed. (Grand Rapids: Zondervan, 1980), 84: "Herod himself founded six cities, Archelaus one village (*komé*), Philip two cities, and Antipas three cities."

40. This entire line of reasoning argues against the Galilean isolationism of Freyne, *Galilee from Alexander the Great to Hadrian*. Note that Wayne Meeks can say "urbanization became the means of hel-lenization" in his discussion of Philip and Alexander the Great, *The First Urban Christians: The Social World of the Apostle Paul* (New Haven: Yale University Press, 1983), 11. It follows that Hellenization implies urbanization.

41. Lee I. Levine, *Caesarea Under Roman Rule* (Leiden: E. J. Brill, 1975), 19. The city as a symbol of power is often under discussion in New World archaeology. See, for example, D. A. Freidel, "Civilization as a state of mind: the cultural evolution of the lowland Maya," in *The Transition to Statehood in the New World*, ed. G. D. Jones and R. R. Kautz (Cambridge: Cambridge University Press, 1981), 188-277.

42. Levine, *Caesarea*, 20.

43. See, for example, the list for Sepphoris in J. Andrew Overman, "Who Were the First Urban Christians? Urbanization in Galilee in the First Century," in *Society for Biblical Literature 1988 Seminar Papers*, ed. David J. Lull (Atlanta: Scholars Press, 1988), 164.

44. James L. Kinneavy, *Greek Rhetorical Origins of Christian Faith: An Inquiry* (New York and Oxford: Oxford University Press, 1987), 78. Gerd Theissen asserts that the gentile gymnasia would have weakened the position of Jerusalem because of a liberalization of its culture; therefore the Maccabees could not allow gymnasia, *Sociology of Early Palestinian Christianity*, 69. While this argument may pertain in the Maccabean period, it is hard to maintain in the face of Herod's building of a theatre and a hippodrome within the holy city.

45. Ibid.

46. See J. B. Ward-Perkins, *Cities of Ancient Greece and Rome: Planning in Classical Antiquity* (New York: George Braziller, 1974). Since peace and order were such watchwords of the Augustan age, we would expect the Herods to imitate the symbols of peace and order (Stam-

baugh, *Ancient Roman City*, 49). The urban symbols of peace and order built by Augustus in Rome include the Forum Augustum, the Porticus Octaviae, the Temple of Apollo Palatinus, and the Arcus Augusti. In 29 B.C.E., Augustus dedicated the Temple of the Deified Julius and the Curia and Chalcidicum. In the Forum Romanum, he erected a new triple-spanned commemorative arch (ibid., 50-51). It is at least reasonable to construct a testable hypothesis that archaeology of the Herodian age in Galilee and Judea should recover similar architectural symbols of peace and order, perhaps at Paneas-Caesarea Phillipi if not Caesarea or Sebasté.

47. John Wilinson, *Jerusalem as Jesus Knew It: Archaeology as Evidence* (London: Thames & Hudson, 1978), 53-65; Eric M. Meyers and James F. Strange, *Archaeology, the Rabbis, and Early Christianity* (Nashville: Abingdon Press, 1981), 49-56.

48. I owe this insight to a remark of Lee I. Levine in *Recent Archaeology in the Land of Israel*, ed. Benjamin Mazar and Hershel Shanks (Washington, D.C.: Biblical Archaeology Society, 1981), 84, in his essay, "Archaeological Discoveries from the Greco-Roman Era," 75-87.

49. Alan Segal, "Theatres in Eretz-Israel in the Roman-Byzantine Period," *Eretz-Israel* 19, 106-24 (Hebrew); English summary, 75-76. An amphitheater or circus has also been unearthed at Beth Shean and an amphitheater, perhaps for gladiatorial combat, has appeared at ancient Eleutheropolis. See Amos Kloner, "The Roman Ampitheatre at Beth Guvrin: Preliminary Report," *Israel Exploration Journal* 38 (1988): 15-24.

50. Stambaugh, *Ancient Roman City*, ad loc.

51. Frank E. Brown, *Roman Architecture* (New York: George Braziller, 1961), 28-29, pl. 45.

52. R. Meiggs, *Roman Ostia*, 2d ed. (Oxford: Oxford University Press, 1989).

53. L. Richardson, Jr., *Pompeii: An Architectural History* (Baltimore: John Hopkins University Press, 1989), 77.

54. Ibid., 131-34.

55. See, for example, Levine, *Caesarea*, 27-29. One must also mention baths as a quintessential Roman institution.

56. Meshorer, *City Coins of Eretz-Israel*, 7, does not discuss the reality of the temples on coins. For the position that temples on city coins do not necessarily imply the actual existence of the temples, see Martin Goodman, *State and Society in Roman Galilee, A.D. 132-212* (Totowa: Rowan & Allenheld, 1983), 46. On the other hand, Goodman seems to understand that Roman temples are part of the "Roman overlay," for he speaks of the building of the Hadrianeum in Tiberias as a "political act," 46.

57. Martin Goodman, *The Ruling Class of Judea: The Origins of the Jewish Revolt against Rome A.D. 66-70* (Cambridge: Cambridge University Press, 1987). For the view that a Jewish peasantry was oppressed both by Rome and by a Jewish (urban) aristocracy, see Richard A.

Horsley and John S. Hanson, *Bandits, Prophets, and Messiahs: Popular Movements at the Time of Jesus* (San Francisco: Harper & Row, 1985).

58. Adolf Büchler, *The Political and Social Leaders of the Jewish Community of Sepphoris in the Second and Third Centuries* (London: Jews' College Publication 1, 1909), 21-26. Büchler believes that local Jewish judges could render verdicts according to Roman law or according to Torah.

59. A. N. Sherwin-White, *Roman Society and Roman Law in the New Testament* (Oxford: Oxford University Press, 1963), 133. Josephus, for example, appointed seventy elders as magistrates for both Galilees when the Roman court system presumably failed (*War* 2.571).

60. Goodman, *Ruling Class of Judea*, 70f.

61. G. Alon, *The Jews in their Land in the Talmudic Age (70-640 C.E.)*, 2 vols. (Jerusalem, 1890-1894), 196-205; Emil Schürer, *The History of the Jewish People in the Age of Jesus Christ (175 B.C. - A.D. 135)*, vol. 2, rev. G. Vermes, F. Millar, M. Black (Edinburgh: T & T Clark, 1979), 199-236 (on the Sanhedrin).

62. See the discussion in ibid., 415-16. See also Wilhelm Bacher, *Die Agada der Tannaitin*, vol. 1 (Strasbourg: K. J. Trubner, 1903).

63. There seems to be a developing consensus that the "synagogue" in the first century C.E. was not yet a building dedicated to one distinctive purpose. For a brief summary of recent research, see Moshe Dothan, "Research on Ancient Synagogues in the Land of Israel," in Mazar and Shanks, *Recent Archaeology in the Land of Israel* , 89-96. On the origins of the synagogue, see Lee I. Levine, "Ancient Synagogues —A Historical Introduction," in Lee I. Levine, ed., *Ancient Synagogues Revealed* (Jerusalem: The Hebrew University, 1981), 1-10.

64. James F. Strange, Dennis E. Groh, and T. R. W. Longstaff, "Sepphoris (Zippori), 1987," Notes and News, *Israel Exploration Journal* 38/3 (1988): 188-90; idem, "Sepphoris (Zippori), 1988," Notes and News, *Israel Exploration Journal* 34 (1984): 51-52; James F. Strange and T. R. W. Longstaff, "Sepphoris (Zippori)—Survey, 1984," Notes and News, *Israel Exploration Journal* 34 (1984): 269-70; idem, "Sepphoris (Zippori, 1985 (II)," Notes and News, *Israel Exploration Journal* 35 (1985): 297-99; idem, "Sepphoris (Zippori), 1986 (II)," Notes and News, *Israel Exploration Journal* 37/4 (1987):278-80. Also Eric M. Meyers, Carol L. Meyers, and Ehud Netzer, "Sepphoris (Zippori), 1985 (I)," *Israel Exploration Journal* 35 (1985): 295-97; idem, "Sepphoris (Zippori), 1986 — Joint Sepphoris Project," *Israel Exploration Journal* 37/4 (1987): 275-78.

65. The most comprehensive study of this inscription is in F. Hüttenmeister and G. Reeg, *Die Antiken Synagogen in Israel*, vol. 1 (Wiesbaden: Reichert, 1977), 400-18. The authors give seven readings of the Greek inscription with a line by line commentary, 406-407, resulting in a confused reading. The most recent study is that of Lea Roth-Gerson, *The Greek Inscriptions from the Synagogues in Eretz-Israel* (Jerusalem: Yad Ben Zvi, 1987): 105-10 (Hebrew).

66. Eric M. Meyers, Carol L. Meyers, and Ehud Netzer, "Sepphoris — 'Ornament of All Galilee,'" *Biblical Archaeologist* 49/1 (1986): 4-19; idem, "A Mansion in the Sepphoris Acropolis and Its Splendid Mosaic," *Qadmoniot* 21 (1988): 87-99, six photographs and plans (Hebrew); Reina Talmon and Zev Weiss, "'Long Live Dionysos!' in the Mosaic of Sepphoris," *Qadmoniot* 21 (1988): 93-99, with eleven photographs.

67. Eliezer L. Sukenik, "Some Remains of Sepphoris," *Tarbiz* 3 (1932): 107-109. See also idem, "Two Jewish Tombstones from Sepphoris," *Bulletin of the Jewish Palestine Exploration Society* 12/6 (1945): 62-64 (Hebrew).

68. Leroy Waterman, et al., *Preliminary Report of the University of Michigan Excavations at Sepphoris, Palestine, in 1931* (Ann Arbor: University of Michigan Press, 1937), 6-12.

69. Gideon Sjoberg, *The Pre-Industrial City* (New York: Macmillan, 1960), 11; see also D. I. Scargill, *The Form of Cities*, Urban and Social Geography Series (London: Bell & Hyman, 1979), 183. Wayne Meeks echoes the point that Paul had an "urban strategy," *First Urban Christians*, 11.

70. D. W. Bösen, *Galiläa als Lebensraum und Wirkungsfeld Jesus* (Freiburg: Herder, 1985); Freyne, *Galilee, Jesus, and the Gospels*, 70-89; Douglas R. Edwards, "First-Century Urban/Rural Relations in Lower Galilee: Exploring the Archaeological and Literary Evidence," in *Society of Biblical Literature 1988 Seminar Papers*, ed. David J. Lull (Atlanta: Scholars Press, 1988), 169-82.

71. Avi-Yonah has noted the importance of Capernaum as a village with a customs office; see *The Holy Land*, 138, repeated in Michael Avi-Yonah, *Gazetteer of Roman Palestine*, Qedem 5 (Jerusalem: The Hebrew University, 1976), 46. Capernaum was a tax collection site because of its situation on the route from Damascus to the Mediterranean, according to Hoehner, *Herod Antipas*, 76. Joseph Blenkinsopp asserts the contrary view that Capernaum was relatively insignificant in his essay, "The Roman Period (to ca. A.D. 324)," in *Excavations at Capernaum*, vol. 1: 1978-1982, ed. Vassilios Tzaferis (Winona Lake, Ind.: Eisenbrauns, 1989), 201-12.

72. Ibid., Plan I.

73. For a full discussion of the ancient notices and a summary discussion of archaeology at the site of Tell Hum before the Franciscan excavations, see Clemens Kopp, *The Holy Places of the Gospels* (Freiburg: Herder; Montreal: Palm Publishers, 1963), 171-77. For a popular but nearly complete discussion, see Stanislao Loffreda, *Recovering Capharnaum*, Studium Biblicum Franciscanum Guides 1 (Jerusalem: Custodia Terra Sancta, 1985).

74. b. Eruv. 13b gives a tradition in the name of R. Abba about the unresolved discussions in the *beth ha-midrash* between pupils of Shammai and the pupils of Hillel. It is possible to argue that this is anachronistic. On the other hand, y. Shab. 16:8-15d speaks of Yohanan

b. Zakkai, famous for his pupils in Jerusalem, who lived part of his life at Arav in Galilee, but who suffered frustration in not being able to attract cases. See Jacob Neusner, *Development of a Legend: Studies on the Traditions Concerning Yohanan ben Zakkai* (Leiden: E. J. Brill, 1970), 133. Neusner thinks the tradition about Yohanan's frustration is wholly the invention of R. Ulla. In this Q passage, it seems likely that rabbinical "tertiary" education is under discussion, particularly in view of teaching the "least" of the commandments, which sounds like an advanced curriculum. See the remarks of Goodman, *State and Society*, 75f. We know very little about village schools, but a Greek inscription from Bakousa near Antioch may refer to a village school. If so, it is the only recorded school outside the ancient literature. See Harper, "Village Administration," 153.

75. Büchler, *Political and Social Leaders*, 68-78.

76. Sean Freyne thinks that this verse, among others, reveals a society in which litigation is an everyday occurrence (*Galilee, Jesus, and the Gospels*, 73). If so, it is all the more striking, as then we have a regular demand for a court system and all it entails. Martin Goodman (*State and Society*, 101, 126) argues that villages *did* have courts. Yet he is speaking of rich men with idle time to serve as judges. It is important to note that no inscriptions from Syria locate judges in villages, though we have a variety of village officials. See Harper, "Village Administration," 116-41. On second- and third-century judges at Sepphoris, see Büchler, *Political and Social Leaders*, 21-23.

77. Goodman, *State and Society*, 131.

78. On taxation in Galilee, see Hoehner, *Herod Antipas*, 73-79.

79. Goodman, *State and Society*, 131.

80. Freyne reminds us that the narrator of the Gospel of Matthew takes it for granted that gentiles have easy access to Galilee (*Galilee, Jesus, and the Gospels*, 54, and more often). Goodman cites a famous text (t. Sheb. 3:6) in which R. Reuben spoke with a philosopher in Tiberias on a Sabbath (*State and Society*, 74).

81. Richard A. Batey, "Jesus and the Theatre," *New Testament Studies* 30 (October 1984): 563-74.

82. Sounding the trumpet before almsgiving is not found in Jewish tradition. See Samuel Tobias Lachs, *A Rabbinic Commentary on the New Testament: The Gospels of Matthew, Mark, and Luke* (Hoboken: Ktav, 1987), 112-15. Lachs offers an ingenuous solution in which "trumpet" translates *shofar* with the meaning of "a container shaped in the form of a horn," 112. But on p. 113, Lachs asks, "What is hypocritical about sounding a trumpet? It is vulgar and ostentatious but not hypocrytical. The hypocrite in Greek usage was an actor and a showman. If one pretended to drop money into the *zedagah* box or claimed that he gave more than he actually did, then this would fit the role of the hypocrite and make other explanations of the term superfluous."

83. On the passage in the Yerushalmi, see Jacob Neusner, *The Talmud of the Land of Israel: A Preliminary Translation and Explanation*, vol. 22

(Chicago: University of Chicago Press, 1985), 51-54. On the meaning of *platea* (a Greek loan word) in Plautus, see Stambaugh, *Ancient Roman City*, 35. For the possible meaning of plazas, see 188. On the problem of the meaning of *platea* in western Roman contexts, see F. W. Harsh, "'Angiportum,' 'Platea,' and 'Vicus,'" *Classical Philology* 32 (1937): 44-58, esp. 56. "The main thoroughfares (running from the gates of the city to the forum... are usually termed *plateai*; the cross-streets, *angiporta.*" Johannes P. Louw, Eugene A. Nida, et al., eds., *Greek-English Lexicon of the New Testament Based on Semantic Domains*, vol. 1 (New York: United Bible Societies, 1988), 1.103, 19; Walter Bauer, William F. Arndt, and F. Wilbur Gingrich, *A Greek-English Lexicon of the New Testament and Other Early Christian Literature* (Chicago: University of Chicago Press, 1957), 672. Incidentally, when I hear this passage in Matthew through the ears of Roman culture overlaying a local Jewish culture, I laugh. It is funny to think that praying in public is like actors drumming up business for the next play.

84. See above, n.31. It must also be allowed that this figure could be a literary construct of Matthew's drawn from his own, perhaps non-Galilean, urban environment.

85. Lightfoot could cite two Jewish texts to the effect that excessive fasting led to a "black" face, but this does not fit the context. John Lightfoot, *A Commentary on the New Testament from the Talmud and Hebraica* (Peabody, Mass.: Hendrickson, 1979) = *Horai Hebraicai et Talmudicai*, vol. 2 (Oxford: Oxford University Press, 1859), 154; Lachs, *A Rabbinic Commentary*, 124-25.

86. Stambaugh, *Ancient Roman City*, 229. I again find this a humorous picture. When I think of fasting and of doing it with a face painted like a mime, that has humor.

87. Freyne thinks this is an image of a walled city on a mountain, perhaps as at the beginning of the sermon (Matt. 5:14). But Freyne wants this to be a rural, if not a pilgrimage motif (*Galilee, Jesus and the Gospels*, 74). The point is that Jesus (or Matthew) apparently expects his audience to know the image, for they see walled cities daily, even if they do not visit them daily.

88. Miller, "Studies in the history and Traditions of Sepphorit," 29, insists that the rabbinic references to the "old fort" at Sepphoris refer to a Jewish garrison.

89. Contra Freyne, *Galilee, Jesus, and the Gospels*, 74.

90. b. Erub. 29a: "Raba said, 'I am in the condition of Ben Azzai in the markets of Tiberias.'" b. Erub. 54b: "It was said of R. Eleazar that he sat and studied Torah in the lower market of Sepphoris while his linen cloak lay in the upper market of the town." b. Yoma. 11a: "It happened to an Artaban [a Tribune?] who was examining *mezuzoth* in the upper market of Sepphoris..."

91. Ramsay MacMullen, *Roman Social Relations* (New Haven: Yale University Press, 1966), 54, on going to market. See also idem, "Market Days in the Roman Empire," *Phoenis* 24/4 (1970): 333-41; Ian W. J.

Hopkins, "The City Region in Roman Palestine," *Palestine Exploration Quarterly* (1980): 19-32.

92. On the management of estates in Xenophoe and the Mishnah, see Jacob Neusner, *The Economics of the Mishnah* (Chicago: University of Chicago Press, 1990), 26-29.

93. Stambaugh, *Ancient Roman City*, 34.

94. On absentee landlords in the gospels, see Freyne, *Galilee, Jesus, and the Gospels*, 151 (referring to Matt. 21:33). On the householder as the basic building block in Jewish economics, see Neusner, *Economics of the Mishnah*, 114-35.

95. Arye Ben-David, *Talmudische Ökonomie: Die Wirtschaft des jüdische Palästina zur Zeit der Mischna und des Talmud*, vol. 1 (Hildesheim and New York: George Olms, 1974).

96. It is faintly possible that this text refers to the marriage of the king's son, therefore to the foundation of Tiberias. Since the argument is entirely circumstantial, it remains unconvincing. Cf. J. H. A. Hart, "Possible References to the Foundation of Tiberias in the Teaching of Our Lord," *The Expositor*, 8th series, 1 (1911): 74-81.

97. See above, n.64. See also y. Ket. I:1 [I].

98. Bauer, Arndt, Gingrich, *Greek-English Lexicon*, 744.

Chapter 3

Reflections on the Study of Israelite History

J. Maxwell Miller

I begin with some explanation of my topic in view of its inclusion in a volume dealing with the relationship of archaeology and faith. There are two considerations. First, my main interest all along has been the history of biblical times. I regard myself as a historian rather than an archaeologist, and I do archaeology because it provides crucial information relevant to historical research. Second, while archaeological theory and archaeological data may impinge upon one's faith in various ways, perhaps the most obvious way for those of us in the Judeo-Christian tradition has to do with history. The Bible presupposes a very dynamic understanding of history, reports amazing and miraculous events, and offers far-reaching interpretations of these events— theological interpretations which lie at the core of our Judeo-Christian beliefs. Is there any way to verify these fantastic historical claims? What does archaeology say? Does archaeology support the biblical account of ancient Israel's history?

QUESTIONS FOR FAITH

Before focusing on historical issues, let me give just one example of other ways that archaeology may impinge on one's faith. Perhaps I should admit that this example is confessional. This is another way, quite apart from its implications for my research in Israelite history, that archaeology forces me to ponder questions of ultimate significance.

Most of our written records from ancient times are the product of, and thus reflect the attitudes of, upper-class society. Archaeology is more democratic. While uncovering royal palaces and temples, we can also excavate in the poorest sections of town. Archaeology reminds us of how the masses have lived throughout the ages, in other words, what it was like to live in a dismal Palestinian village during the early Iron Age, for example, while King Solomon was "lying beside the still waters" with his "cup running over." The bottom line is this: the life style that Solomon enjoyed, and the even more comfortable lifestyle that we educated westerners take for granted today, is a radical exception to the human norm. The normal human state throughout the ages, I think it correct to say, has been physical misery—marginal subsistence living with minimal protection against the cold and heat of the ever changing seasons, uncertain food supply even in the best of times, and the constant threat of famine and disease. And that is to say nothing of social ills and political oppressions which often have exacerbated the misery.

We know nothing about the psalmist who proclaimed that God created humans "a little less than the angels," but I will wager that he was not a peasant farmer. Certainly the so-called Priestly writer of Genesis 1 was reflecting an elitist attitude when he asserted that God created us in the divine image and charged us to "be fruitful and multiply, and fill the earth and subdue it." The Yahwist was more in touch with the realities of the human condition. If anything, humans are, in his opinion, the least blessed of all the creatures. Throughout the ages, countless of our nameless predecessors have struggled against the obstinate forces of nature, scratched out just enough food from the earth's crust to survive a short while, endured fear, pain, and sorrow, and died.

What does all of this mean? What kind of world is this in which millions of babies from every generation die the painful death of starvation and disease before reaching even their second birthday? And what am I to make of the fact that I was born at such a luxurious time and place in the sweep of human history and allowed, with the help of archaeology, to look back over our past? In short, archaeology raises again, for me, the theodicy question: How could a good and just God be responsible for such a world? At the same time, it renders unsatisfactory the standard answers, especially the social gospel answer: "He has no hands but our hands . . . get busy and change the situation." As a historian and an archaeologist, I find myself reflecting on the human misery that cannot be changed because it has already happened. Neither do I find Jesus' passing remark about having "the poor with you always" very encouraging.

ARCHAEOLOGY AND THE
MODERN HISTORIAN OF ISRAEL

Turning now to matters of history, my comments will focus on two crucial questions: Is it appropriate or realistic for a modern historian to attempt to write a critical history of ancient Israel? And if so, where does one begin? What can be said about the origin of the Israelites, in other words, and what are the earliest archaeological traces of their presence? Let me begin by describing two opposing (and in my opinion extreme) positions, both of which seem to imply a negative answer to the first question regarding the appropriateness of attempting to write a history of ancient Israel.

The first is the position of those who hold the Bible itself, as is, to be a completely accurate and satisfactory account of

Israel's past. This position short-circuits normal historical investigation, if for no other reason than that it conflicts with one of the basic tenets of modern historiography—namely, that the historian must always approach his or her sources with a critical spirit, with some degree of skepticism. Illustrating this position at the popular level, a typical response to any talk of contradictions or other apparent historical problems in the biblical record is: one must accept it on faith. Translated, that means that one should not press the historical questions. Let them be!

A corresponding attitude is represented in academic circles by those who presuppose at the outset of their research that any apparent contradictions in the biblical record are only apparent and that all extrabiblical evidence will, when interpreted properly, fit the Bible story. For them, therefore, historical research becomes largely an exercise in explaining away contradictions and searching for extrabiblical fits. Membership in the Near East Archaeological Society,[1] for example, which was founded by a circle of evangelical scholars, presupposes agreement with the following statement of faith (which is presented for signature on the membership form): "The Bible alone and the Bible in its entirety is the word of God written, and therefore inerrant in the autographs." Some of the members of this society are accomplished archaeologists in terms of data-collecting techniques, which means that the society bulletin often includes valuable information that other archaeologists take seriously. However, collecting data and interpreting data are two different things. No interpretations that conflict with the Bible ever find their way into the *Near East Archaeological Society Bulletin*, and other archaeologists also take that into account.

The second position, representing an opposite extreme, is that of those who are so skeptical regarding the whole enterprise of historiography or the possibility of extracting authentic historical information from the Bible that they disparage altogether any research into the history of ancient

Israel. First, these skeptics point to the overriding epistemological and methodological dilemmas that plague all
historians, even historians of more recent times. Historians
depend heavily on the "analogy" principle, for example. We
assume that the past was totally analogous with the present
and interpret past events accordingly. To see how this works
in treatments of Israelite history, remember that the Bible
presupposes a dynamic natural world into which God, from
time to time, intrudes upon human affairs. It is a world with
waters rolling back, burning bushes, and axheads floating.
God directs the course of history by simultaneously instruct-
ing Moses, regulating Pharaoh's heart, and bringing
unnatural disasters upon Egypt. God hands down laws on
Mount Sinai, and sends angels to defend Jerusalem against
Sennacherib's massive army.

 Modern historians perceive the world to be more orderly,
on the other hand; and another of the standard tenets of
modern historiography is that any natural or historical
phenomenon can be explained without reference to overt
divine involvement. Thus we modern historians systemati-
cally revise the biblical narratives even as we draw upon
them for historical information. Specifically, we bring them
into line with the world as we perceive it. We leave out the
miracles, for example, or spill a lot of ink explaining how they
really could have happened in the orderly world as we
understand it. We offer different explanations for historical
developments which do not involve "God talk." This is the
analogy principle at work.

 But can we assume that the past was continuous with the
present in every way? Is there not at least the theoretical
possibility that some past events were unique and thus simply not explainable on analogy with the present order? And
how far can we trust our understanding of the present order?
Epistemological questions of this sort challenge the very
foundations of modern historiography.

 Then, even if we could get past the overriding epistemological dilemmas, there is the problem of the historian's

individual subjectivity. If we have learned anything in the present century, it is that historians themselves are caught in history. Our best shots at objectivity inevitably reflect the assumptions, values, and special interests of our peer groups, as well as our individual quirks. Probably it is not an overstatement to say that any history book reveals as much about its author as it does about the period treated.

When it comes to a history of ancient Israel, for example, the historian's religious training and theological perspective very likely will be involved. I have already suggested, for example, that there is a direct connection between the fact that the members of the Near East Archaeological Society begin with the conviction of biblical inerrancy and the fact that none of the archaeological interpretations presented in their bulletin ever conflict with the Bible story. But it is not only the inerrancy crowd that comes into consideration here. Anyone who espouses a theology that places even some emphasis on biblical authority almost certainly will treat many aspects of biblical history differently from one who is reacting against a fundamentalist upbringing. Let me emphasize: I am not suggesting that subjectivity is a special problem for religiously committed or reactionary scholars. All historians work from some philosophical or theological base, whether consciously or not. Yet the confessional element is one of the more obvious factors that show up in treatments of Israelite history.

Finally, there is the inevitable dependency/distrust relationship between the historian and his or her sources of information. The historian is dependent on whatever sources are available. But rarely do the sources provide exactly the sort of information the historian wants. And usually there is a degree of bias involved, or some other problem which renders the source less than absolutely trustworthy.

Our primary source of information for reconstructing the history of ancient Israel, of course, is the Hebrew Bible. Other ancient Near Eastern sources and archaeology augment the biblical record. But these nonbiblical sources really tell us very little about ancient Israel in and of themselves. Not only does the Hebrew Bible supply most of our information, but it provides the context for interpreting the nonbiblical evidence.[2] At the moment, there is heavy emphasis among biblical scholars on the literary artistry and highly crafted literary structure of the biblical narratives. The implication is that these narratives preserve very little authentic historical memory, and that whatever authentic memory may have been preserved is no longer recognizable because it is so deeply embedded in the artistically constructed stories. Accordingly, some contemporary biblical scholars would regard any attempt to write a history of ancient Israel as an inappropriate undertaking—a "lost cause," if you will. Burke Long, for example, warns that one cannot extract history from "a holy book that tells stories."[3]

Thus we have two opposing positions, both of which seem to preclude any depth research into the history of ancient Israel. Most biblical scholars, certainly those of us who focus our research on Israelite history, fall somewhere in between. This "in between" position is not entirely satisfactory from either a theoretical or methodological point of view. But it is where I find myself after following to their logical end the two more extreme positions described above.

Having grown up in a conservative Protestant tradition that places strong emphasis on biblical authority, and having read the Bible closely enough to know that its theological message cannot be easily separated from its historical claims, it was with a tremendous sense of loss, pain, and fear that I first broke that awesome eleventh commandment: "Thou shalt not doubt, for whosoever doubteth anything in the Bible or any aspect of the received faith will burn in hell." Gradually it dawned upon me that doubting is not a sin which one commits, but a natural aspect of intellectual and spiritual growth. By the time I reached my early twenties, moreover, I had decided that, whatever the implications for biblical authority, the Bible does present historical contradictions and inaccuracies, and that I could not perform the mental gymnastics required to think otherwise. In short, I bought into the historical-critical approach to biblical studies.

By the time I reached my early thirties, however, I was becoming increasingly aware that everything is not nailed down in the historical-critical camp either. Specifically, I began to consider the unprovable assumptions and epistemological fallacies underlying modern historiography, the many subjective factors that influence any historian's judgment, and the ineffectiveness of our best critical tools when it comes to recognizing whatever authentic historical memory does survive in our ancient sources. In fact, all of the objections raised above against the feasibility of reconstructing the history of any period, much less the history of ancient Israel, are points that I have raised and elaborated on in earlier occasions. Moreover, I have argued that archaeology does not enable us to make an "end run" around these objections. Archaeological interpretation likewise rests on the analogy principle and involves highly subjective judgments on the part of the interpreter.[4]

Yet I have written a history of Israel in spite of these objections, and I attempt to justify the undertaking on essentially three grounds.[5] First, it is not a question, after all, of whether there was an ancient Israel or whether the Bible provides any relevant historical information at all. The very existence of the Bible is an important item of historical evidence. Second, a large portion of the Bible presents itself as history—narration of sequences of people and events, with explicit historical claims and interpretations. Thus the Bible itself raises, indeed forces, historical questions; and engaging the Bible on its own terms necessarily involves us with these questions. Finally, it is virtually impossible to proceed with other avenues of biblical research without at least some assumptions and notions regarding the history of ancient Israel. The only choice for biblical scholars, therefore, or for any serious reader of the Bible, is whether these assumptions and notions will be informed by careful research or derived by unconscious osmosis from reading the Bible stories.

To illustrate the sort of discussion that unfolds among those of us who take the "in between" route with respect to the extreme positions described above, let us turn to the second question posed at the beginning of this presentation—namely, the question of the origin of the Israelites and the earliest archaeological traces of their presence.

In the early 1960s, when I did my graduate training, W. F. Albright's approach to the history of ancient Israel reigned supreme in the English-speaking world. His approach and main views were expounded in John Bright's *A History of Israel,*[6] which was a standard textbook in seminaries and graduate schools of religion. The only strong competitor was Martin Noth's *Geschichte Israels,*[7] which served as the standard history of Israel for German-speaking scholars.

According to Albright, Israel's history began with the patriarchs (Abraham, Isaac, and Jacob), who could be associated with Amorite movements that occurred in the Fertile Crescent about 2000 B.C.E. Israel took shape as a nation later, at the time of the exodus from Egypt and conquest of Canaan, which Albright believed could be dated during the thirteenth century B.C.E.—that is, at the end of the Late Bronze Age. Israel, therefore, according to the Albright approach, was primarily an ethnic designation, and the earliest archaeological evidence of Israel's presence would be the pattern of city destructions that marked the end of the Late Bronze Age in Palestine.

Martin Noth, skeptical of the historicity of the patriarchs and developing the views of his teacher, Albrecht Alt, took a different tack. The Alt-Noth position had seminomads from the desert fringe gradually settling those parts of Palestine that had been less densely populated during the Bronze Age, consolidating into a twelve-tribe confederacy early in the Iron Age, and emerging as a monarchy under Saul, David, and Solomon around 1000 B.C.E. The tribal confederacy was similar to Greek amphictyonies, in Noth's opinion, and there was no Israelite conquest of Canaan until the first Israelite kings, especially David, extended their realm from the Palestine hill country into the lowlands. From the Alt-Noth perspective, therefore, earliest Israel was more of a cultic and political entity than an ethnic entity. And presumably the earliest archaeological traces would be the early Iron Age villages that emerged in previously less densely populated parts of Palestine—although allowance must be made for the presence of non-Israelite villages in the same areas.

The Albright approach and the Alt-Noth approach had three things in common: (1) Both assumed that the Israelites entered Palestine from the outside. (2) Both saw premonarchical Israel as a tightly-structured twelve-tribe league that spread over most of Palestine. (3) Both thought in terms of a sharp distinction between the Israelites and the Canaanites, at least in early tribal times. The Canaanites had an urban heritage; the Israelites were recent arrivals from the desert. The Canaanites were polytheists whose gods were seen to be active primarily in nature; the Israelites worshiped a god who "acts in history." The Canaanites assumed that monarchy was the normal form of government; the Israelites were a fiercely independent tribal people who looked to their elders for leadership, except when Yahweh designated a temporary, charismatic leader to lead the tribes into battle.

Only mangled remnants of these competing Albright and Alt-Noth views concerning the origin of Israel survive in the current discussion—or at least as far as the cutting-edge literature is concerned. Thomas Thompson[8] and John Van Seters[9] demolished Albright's arguments for the historicity of the patriarchs in the early 1970s, and I am not aware of any serious attempt, certainly not any successful attempt, to recover them for history.[10] As new archaeological evidence became available, it was increasingly apparent that most of it argues against a thirteenth-century conquest.[11] Noth's amphictyony hypothesis likewise collapsed under closer scrutiny.[12]

Also during the 1970s, while the Albright and Alt-Noth views were encountering difficulties, an entirely different model for explaining the origin of Israel began to spread like wildfire among biblical scholars. First advanced by George Mendenhall,[13] but developed by Norman Gottwald[14] (in a somewhat different direction than Mendenhall intended), this has come to be called the "peasants revolt" hypothesis. According to this hypothesis, disturbances broke out all over Palestine at the end of the Late Bronze Age, peasants throwing off the yoke of their Canaanite overlords. Resulting from these widespread peasant revolts and centering primarily in the central Palestinian hill country, there emerged a new socio-religio-political structure called Israel. The city destructions, which Albright had attributed to the invading Israelites, still belonged to the picture, except that now they were associated with internal peasant revolts rather than attributed to invaders from the outside. Also, the distinction between Israelites and Canaanites took a new twist with this hypothesis. The distinction now had to do with religious conversion (Mendenhall) or socio-political ideology (Gottwald). As far as their ethnic origin and cultural heritage was concerned, the earliest Israelites were Canaanites.

This "peasants revolt" hypothesis faded as quickly as it spread, but with lingering influence in two regards. Although the idea of a peasants revolt has fallen by the wayside, the thought that Israel may have emerged in Palestine, essentially from the indigenous population rather than arriving there from somewhere else, remains very appealing. Also, there remains a strong inclination among contemporary scholars to employ sociological models in their efforts to understand the dynamics of how Israel emerged and how the structure of earliest Israelite society would have looked.

THE PRESENT STATE OF THE DISCUSSION

So where does the discussion now stand? Essentially three positions can be identified. First, there are those who place much confidence in the biblical account of Israel's origin and continue the search for some way to correlate it with archaeology. Albrightian in approach, but much more conservative in their use of the biblical materials, leading spokesmen for this position are John Bimson[15] and Bryant Wood.[16] Their program calls for a fifteenth-century exodus-conquest, a radical restructuring of archaeological chronology to accommodate the fifteenth-century date, and explaining away a significant amount of archaeological evidence that still does not fit in spite of the redating and restructuring.[17]

Second, there are those of us (placing myself in this category) who are inclined to believe that Israel emerged by and large from the indigenous population of Palestine at approximately the transition from the Bronze Age to the Iron Age. Yet we suspect that this would have been a gradual and evolutionary process, rather than the result of any sort of conscious revolt.[18] There are different opinions as to exactly what the name "Israel" would have designated in the early stages of the process, but there is growing agreement that it would have pertained in some way to the northcentral Palestinian hill country. Gösta Ahlström thinks that it was primarily a geographical designation for this area.[19] In my opinion, a stronger case can be made that it referred to a cluster of tribes centered in that area and dominated by the tribe of Ephraim.[20] In either case, the Early Iron Age villages in the northcentral hill country would represent early Israelite society—still with the qualification that there were also villages in that area which the biblical narrators regarded as non-Israelite, and that archaeologists have no way of determining which were which.

The third position is similar to the second except, in my opinion, its proponents are inclined toward muddled historio-graphical methodology and overconfidence in the scientific certainty of their conclusions. Typically, these scholars express strong disregard for the Hebrew Bible as a source of historical information and take an equally dim view of any historical research that relies heavily on literary-critical methodologies. It is not surprising, therefore, since the name "Israel" rarely occurs in ancient sources outside the Hebrew Bible, that these scholars tend to beg the fundamental questions, such as when exactly Israel emerged on the scene of history, what exactly Israel was, and where exactly the Israelites settled. Nevertheless, they proceed with confidence to spell out the socio-economics of Israel's origin[21] or to trace the emergence and spread of early Israelite society through archaeology.[22] In effect, they begin with certain unexamined assumptions that were left over from earlier stages of the discussion and that derive ultimately from the Hebrew Bible, regardless of their pronouncements to the contrary, and end up using "Israel" as an all-inclusive term for anyone living in (or within reasonable proximity to) the Palestinian hill country during the Early Iron Age.

CONCLUSION

To summarize, there is a wide range of opinion among contemporary scholars regarding the historical reliability of the Bible. Some, like John Bimson and Brian Wood, are so confident of its accuracy that they are willing to shift archaeological chronology in order to bring it into line with the Bible story. Others, like Burk Long, regard the Bible as essentially useless for the historian's purposes. It is "a holy book that tells stories." Most biblical scholars, certainly those of us who attempt to write critical histories of ancient Israel, fall somewhere in between. We proceed with confidence that the Bible does preserve authentic historical memory, yet recognize that this memory is embedded in narratives that rarely can be taken at face value. Where we fall between the opposite extremes of total confidence and total skepticism, and the methods we use to extract authentic memory from legend, theology, or whatever, makes for the differences in the histories that we write.

NOTES

1. The Near East Archaeology Society (2313 E. 20th St., Joplin, Mo. 64804) publishes the *Near East Archaeological Society Bulletin and Newsletter*.

2. I expanded on this point in a paper titled, "Is It Possible to Write a History of Ancient Israel Without Relying on the Hebrew Bible?" *The Fabric of History: Text, Artifact and Israel's Past*, ed., D.V. Edelman. JSOT Supplement 127 (Sheffield: Sheffield Academic Press).

3. Burke O. Long, "On Finding the Hidden Premises," *Journal for the Study of the Old Testament* 39 (1987): 10-14.

4. See especially *The Old Testament and the Historian* (Philadelphia/London: Fortress/SPCK, 1976); "Biblical History as a Discipline," *Biblical Archaeologist* 45 (1982): 211-16; and "Old Testament History and Archaeology," *Biblical Archaeologist* 49 (1987): 51-62.

5. See especially "In Defense of Writing a History of Israel," *Journal for the Study of the Old Testament* 39 (1987): 10-14.

6. John Bright, *A History of Israel* (Philadelphia/London: Westminster Press/SCM Press, 1959, 1972, 1981).

7. Martin Noth, *Geschichte Israels* (Göttingen: Vandenhoeck & Ruprecht, 1950, 1954); ET *The History of Israel* (London/New York: A & C Black/Harper & Row, 1960).

8. Thomas L. Thompson, "The Historicity of the Patriarchal Narratives," *Beihefte zur Zeitschrift für die alttestamentliche Wissenschaft* 133 (1974).

9. John Van Seters, *Abraham in History and Tradition* (New Haven: Yale University Press, 1975).

10. See also my observations in "The Patriarchs and Extra-Biblical Sources: A Response," *Journal for the Study of the Old Testament* (1977): 62-66; and "W. F. Albright and Historical Reconstruction," *Biblical Archaeologist* 42 (1979): 37-47.

11. See especially M. Weippert, *Die Landnahme der israelitischen Stämme in der neueren wissenschaftlichen Diskussion*, Forschungen zur Religion und Literatur des Alten und Neuen Testaments 92 (Göttingen: Vandenhoeck & Ruprecht,1967); ET *The Settlement of the Israelite Tribes: A Critical Survey of Recent Scholarly Debate*, Studies in Biblical Theology II/21 (London: SCM Press, 1971). Also J. M. Miller, "Archaeology and the Israelite Conquest of Canaan: Some Methodological Considerations," *Palestine Exploration Quarterly* 109 (1977): 87-93; and "The Israelite Occupation of Canaan," chap. 4 of John H. Hayes and J. M. Miller, *Israelite and Judean History* (London/Philadelphia: SCM/Westminster, 1977).

12. See especially A. D. H. Mayes, *Israel in the Period of the Judges*, Studies in Biblical Theology II/29 (London: SCM Press, 1974).

13. G. E. Mendenhall, "The Hebrew Conquest of Palestine," *Biblical Archaeologist* 25 (1962): 66-87.

14. N. K. Gottwald, *The Tribes of Yahweh: A Sociology of Liberated Israel, 1250-1050 BCE* (London: SCM Press, 1979).

15. John Bimson, "Redating the Exodus and Conquest," *Journal for the Study of the Old Testament*, Supplement 5 (1978).

16. Bryant G. Wood, "Did the Israelites Conquer Jericho: A New Look at the Archaeological Evidence," *Biblical Archaeology Review* 16 (1990): 44-59.

17. I examined in more detail the approach championed by Bimson and Wood in a paper titled, "The Witness of Ai." This paper was presented in a 1988 symposium on the topic, "Who was the Pharaoh of the Exodus?" sponsored by the Near East Archaeological Society. Plans are underway to publish all of the papers presented at the symposium in single volume.

18. See my discussion of Israelite origins in chap. 2 of J. M. Miller and J. H. Hayes, *A History of Ancient Israel and Judah* (Philadelphia/London: Westminster Press/SCM Press, 1986).

19. Gösta W. Ahlström, *Who Were the Israelites?* (Winona Lake, Ind.: Eisenbrauns, 1986).

20. See especially chap. 3 of Miller and Hayes, *History of Ancient Israel and Judah*.

21. E.g., R. B. Coote and K. W. Whitelam, *The Emergence of Early Israel in Historical Perspective*, The Social World of Biblical Antiquity Series (Sheffield: Almond Press, 1987).

22. E.g., Israel Finkelstein, *The Archaeology of the Israelite Settlement* (Jerusalem: Israel Exploration Society, 1988).

Chapter 4

The Archaeology of Palestine and the Archaeology of Faith:

Between a Rock
and a Hard Place

W. Waite Willis, Jr.

There is surely an oddity in my participation in
the subject matter of this volume. For I am by training neither
an archaeologist nor a biblical scholar, but a theologian. This
means that I must keep in mind Socrates's injunction "Know
thyself" (Plato, *Phdr.* 229d-230a, *Tim.* 29 c-d). For Socrates this
command did not have to do with our modern psychological
notions of self-analysis. Rather, "Know thyself" advises the
recognition of the limitation of human beings in relation to
the gods. This is my situation precisely. I, a theologian, find
myself inhabiting the same space as some of the gods of
biblical archaeology and history, with scholars who are on
the cutting (or rather digging) edge of archaeological and
historical work.

Nevertheless, reading in the areas of archaeology and history is salutary for the theologian. For the theologian generally seeks for the meaning of the Bible and faith, and often this is done with little regard for the discoveries of the archaeologist and the reconstructions of the historian. The attitude of the theologian can be demonstrated by a story about Karl Barth, the greatest of the modern theologians. After Barth gave a lecture on temptation and sin in which he referred to the Genesis 3 story, a member of the audience asked, "Did the snake actually speak to Eve in the Garden of Eden?" Barth, in good theological fashion, attempted to circumvent a direct answer, but the audience continued to press him. Barth finally replied, "I don't care whether or not the snake spoke to Eve; I'm only interested in what the snake said." However, Barth knew, as every theologian must, that if theology is to be relevant, it must be done with open eyes. It must take into account the issues that areas of study such as archaeology raise for us.

THE BASIC QUESTION

The central issue presented to faith by archaeology is not new or unique. It is a foundational question of the faith, the question of the relationship of faith to history.[1] What in the Bible should one believe? How can one trust the biblical record in light of scholarly analysis? Anyone who has taught an introductory course on the Bible has heard this question. Jonathan Z. Smith, Professor of Humanities at the University of Chicago, claims that every introductory course involves "white lies." The professor, in the name of simplification, ends up "treating theories as if they were facts."[2] However, no amount of white lying can prevent students from struggling when they are confronted with issues in biblical studies, such as questions of authorship, ancient cosmology and demonology, internal contradictions in fact and theology, stories of illicit sexuality and murder, textual variants and the complex process of canonization, to name only a few.

Theologians have the sophistication to respond to many of these questions. But when studying the results of archaeological work, the question arises once again. What does the archaeology of Palestine mean to faith? What is faith to trust when archaeology has at best a mixed relationship with the Bible, the primary text of faith? Where does faith invest itself when archaeology, while supporting some claims of the Bible, tends to call into question many (and is as silent as stone about other) central biblical events and persons?

Persons of the Jewish and Christian faiths find themselves between a rock and a hard place. The Bible speaks of a God who is active in the history of certain supposedly actual persons, places, and events. The archaeologist, then, ought to be able to find evidence not that God was at work in these times and places but that supports the reality of these events. However, archaeology finds no trace of many biblical events and finds evidence that clearly contradicts others. If the persons, places, and events are not real, then how can God be active in them? How trustworthy is the biblical claim that God is present in this history when the narrated events are not factually accurate, or appear not to have taken place, or have left no trace and therefore cannot be determined to have been events at all? The believer is caught between the rock of the biblical claim and the hard place of the archaeological contradiction.

Faith in the historical character of God's work leads one to archaeological work. Archaeological work, on the other hand, calls into question some of the foundational events where God has supposedly worked. This situation between the rock and the hard place forces the theologian and the believer back to a reexamination of faith, to an archaeology of faith itself.

THE INCARNATING GOD OF THE BIBLE

If the Bible spoke only of a God who was active in the heavens in eternity, then archaeology would not present an

issue for biblical faith. For heavenly works produce no earth-
ly artifacts to dig up. The Bible, however, presents a narrative
of a God who is open to the world. The God of the Bible does
not remain isolated, locked in heaven, but reaches out to
communicate the divine self to human beings, to identify
with them in their concrete historical existence in order to
bring them into relationship with, and allow them to participate in, the divine life. This saving self-communication of
God does not take place primarily in supernatural, glorious
intrusions into the world, but through ordinary persons and
historical events. Certainly, in the Bible the revelatory, saving
events are frequently pictured as being accompanied by
extraordinary occurrences. But these occurrences are never,
finally, what is important. What is significant is that God has
acted in that certain place, at that certain time, with those
certain persons. For example, in the story of Moses' encounter with God at Mt. Horeb, the burning bush itself is not
of central importance, but that God has identified with Israel
and called Moses to act for God in the liberation of the people
is. The Bible discloses what we may call the incarnational
character of its God, a God who continuously binds the
divine self to humanity and human history.

The New Testament represents the man Jesus as the
center and primary point of the work of this incarnating God.
All the writers somehow see the history of Jesus as God's
work in the world. This Jesus who was born of a woman, was
raised in Nazareth, moved to Capernaum, gathered disciples, taught crowds of people in Galilee, journeyed to
Jerusalem, was rejected by the religious establishment, was
put to death by the Roman prefect Pontius Pilate—this Jew
who lived between 5 B.C.E. and 30 C.E., who was part of the
history of Palestine of the first century—this human being
was somehow God's revelation and salvation.

In Philippians 2, one of the earliest works of the New
Testament, Paul speaks of this incarnational event found in
Jesus in terms of *kenosis*, self-emptying. Using what was
probably an even earlier Christian hymn,[3] Paul writes of the

one who was equal to God but who "emptied himself, taking the form of a slave, being born in human likeness" (NRSV). In the Fourth Gospel, Jesus is explicitly proclaimed as the incarnation of the divine Word. But even in the earliest gospel, Mark, where incarnation is not explicitly stated, it is clear that God's salvation is made present in the life and, particularly, in the suffering and death of this Jesus. Furthermore, the New Testament writers want to correct any tendency that might suggest that Jesus was not really human. So they fight against docetism, the widely held belief that Jesus only appeared to be human. The New Testament writers focus on the ordinary human side of Jesus' life. He was born; he eats with people; he has close friends; he attends synagogue and teaches there; he has limits to his knowledge; and most importantly, he suffers and dies as humans do. In Jesus, God has not remained at a distance in a reality that merely seems to be human but has really entered human history with all its banality, joy, and tragedy.

Early Christian thinkers took up this biblical claim, and so Ignatius can speak of the suffering of Jesus as "the passion of my God."[4] Later, Origen more extensively speaks of "God's suffering" in Jesus. The Son obviously suffers, but about the Father, Origen asks, "Does He not also suffer in a certain way?" (Homily VI).[5] Finally, the church developed the doctrine of the Trinity that served to protect the Christian claim that an encounter with Jesus really is a revealing and saving encounter with God. In Jesus, God really is acting in history.

It is not, however, only in the New Testament and in Christian theology that one finds the claim for a God who works in history. In the Hebrew Bible or Old Testament, this claim already appears. The Genesis-2 Kings narrative is the prehistory and history of the people of Israel and how Yahweh has bound himself to and worked in and through these people and events. It is primarily God who is the actor in this story. It is God who calls and leads Abraham and Sarah. It is God who grants Jacob success and who brings good out of

the evil done to Joseph by his brothers. It is God who calls
Moses and God who is responsible for the liberation from
Egypt. It is God who brings victory in the conquest of Canaan
and who raises up judges to lead the people. It is God who
commands Samuel to anoint Saul and then David. It is God
who works through the prophets to call people back to the
covenant. And it is God who takes the people into exile. It is
also God who through the conqueror Cyrus enables the
return to Jerusalem.

This God so identifies with these people and their history
that the divine life is affected by these human events. When
the people are in bondage in Egypt, this God "hears their
cries and knows their oppression" (Exodus 3). In Hosea,
there is a struggle in the divine heart over the pain that divine
judgment brings (Hosea 5). With Jeremiah, God weeps for
the people, the ruin they have brought on the nation, and
their judgment by exile.

It was the perception of God's presence with the people
and participation in their history that led early rabbis to
develop the notion of the Shekinah, God's indwelling with
his people.

> Through his Shekinah God is present in Israel. Together with
> Israel he suffers persecutions. Together with Israel he goes into
> exile as a prisoner. Together with the martyrs he experiences the
> torments of death.[6]

Through this concept the rabbis made it clear that God
really is involved in the history of the people of Israel. Even
here, from the Christian perspective, we meet an incarnating
God.

In these brief comments one can see why the biblical
material leads to, in fact demands, archaeological work.
There are ancient people, places, and events that are the focal
points of God's work, and faith demands that we understand
them as best we can, using every means at our disposal.
Beyond that, it looks as if archaeology ought to be able to
support these biblical claims.

THE ARCHAEOLOGICAL QUEST

It was the perception of the historical character of the biblical narrative that gave—and I believe still continues to give—impetus to Palestinian archaeology. That is not because there are merely some historical locations that need to be investigated, but because these historical places and events are referred to in the Bible as the where and when of God's saving activity. That is, it is the religious imagination, generated by biblical faith, that has motivated the archaeological quest in Palestine. Without this motivation it is difficult to imagine why so much effort has been expended on digging up the "dead and primitive past" of Palestine, which always was "culturally and economically a provincial back-water."[7] As William F. Albright stated it:

> The enduring reason for any special interest in Palestine [is that] nearly all the Hebrew Old Testament is a product of Palestinian soil and Israelite writers, while most of the events which underlie the Greek New Testament took place in the same scared terrain.[8]

G. Ernest Wright put it similarly:

> [Biblical archaeology]must be intelligently concerned with stratigraphy and typology, upon which the method of modern archaeology rests; but its chief concern is not with strata or pots or methodology. Its central and absorbing interest is the understanding and exposition of the scriptures.[9]

For at least some archaeologists, the religious imagination gives rise not merely to an intellectual response to the Bible but a desire to get as near as possible to the places and events that are important for faith. As ancient (as well as modern) religious folk have gone on pilgrimages to the Holy Land to get close to the holy places, archaeologists dig to get closer still to the holy sites. Edward Robinson, a precursor to American archaeology in Palestine, accepted an appointment as professor of biblical literature at Union Theological Seminary in 1837 "only on the condition that he be allowed time for travel in Palestine."[10] In the introduction to the account of his historical geography, which included the successful identification of over a hundred biblical sites, we see the importance he placed on this work in Palestine. Robinson writes, "The following work contains the description of a journey, which had been the object of my ardent wishes, and entered into all my plans of life for more than fifteen years."[11]

Even more explicit on the importance of getting close to events and places because they are biblical are the statements of the contemporary Israeli scholar Ephraim Stern. In an article entitled "The Bible and Israeli Archaeology," Stern maintains that for Israeli archaeologists, the assertion being made by some American archaeologists that Palestinian archaeology should be done independently of biblical studies is unintelligible. He writes,

> For us it is not a cut-and dried subject to be described merely in terms of facts, figures, and plans. Our ties with the Bible are direct and emotional. I would even go so far as to say that all of us dealing with this period in the field are motivated by the desire of experiencing the excitement of excavating a building of a biblical settlement and bringing its contents to light.... This feeling of personal involvement is held by all Israeli archaeologists. ...This is the essence and the main purpose of archaeology, while the professional aspect is only a more or less efficient means of attaining it.[12]

The role of the religious imagination in generating archaeological work goes even beyond motivating persons to find information about the biblical sites and deeper than allowing one to participate in the biblical past. Archaeologists have often gone on to claim that their archaeological data could support the historical claims of the Bible. In this case archaeology becomes an apologetic strategy in support of biblical faith. For the concern becomes the correlation of archaeological discoveries with biblical events and places in order to demonstrate the reliability of the Bible. To state it bluntly, the goal is to prove the Bible is factually correct. This factuality in itself would not produce faith, but if the biblical narrative were historically accurate, there would be grounds for the acceptance of the Bible. In response to higher literary critics such as Julius Wellhausen, who asserted the impossibility of obtaining historical information about the patriarchs from the biblical text, archaeologists responded by pointing to archaeological discoveries.[13] In 1894, Archibald H. Sayce, an Assyriologist at Oxford, responding to the skepticism of higher criticism, used archaeology to support the veracity of the Bible:

> The records of the Old Testament have been confronted with the monuments of the ancient world, wherever this was possible, and their trustworthiness has been tested by a comparison with the latest results of archaeological research.... The evidence of oriental archaeology is on the whole distinctly unfavorable to the pretensions of the "higher criticism." The "apologist" may lose something, but the "higher critic" loses much more.[14]

There were warnings from persons like Francis Brown who, in 1896, was the president of the Society of Biblical Literature. He spoke against the improper use of archaeology "as a conservative ally" in supporting the biblical record.[15] Nevertheless, the use of archaeology in doing just this was frequent in the debate over the Bible. In fact, an appeal to the apologetic usefulness of archaeology in support of the Bible and biblical truth was a central element in the arguments for the founding of the American School of Oriental Research in Jerusalem. In his presidential address, "The Historical Element in the New Testament," to the Society of Biblical Literature in 1895, J. Henry Thayer referred to archaeology's great "promise of usefulness alike to Biblical learning and missionary work...."[16]

This use of the archaeology of Palestine in support of the credibility of the biblical narrative reached its apex in the middle decades of this century in the work of the triumvirate William F. Albright, G. Ernest Wright, and John Bright. The tradition growing out of their work is called the Albright school or Albright-Wright school, or the biblical archaeology movement. Employing new and refined archaeological methods of stratigraphy and ceramic typology, as well as meticulous record keeping, Albright, Wright, and others were able to accumulate greater amounts of data, now better understood and supposedly more precisely dated. They then correlated this growing body of information with the biblical history. While they were aware that they could not substantiate every point of the biblical story, they asserted that the general outline of the biblical narrative could be verified. In his influential book, *God Who Acts*, Wright claimed that the Christian community had no need to fear archaeology, because its discoveries of "errors and discrepancies" in the Bible were a "minor feature" whose "destructive nature" had been "exaggerated and misrepresented." Wright declared, "On the contrary, we today possess a greater confidence in the basic reliability of Biblical History, despite all the problems it has presented, than was possible before the historical and archaeological research of the past century...."[17] Earlier, Albright had already claimed that "Biblical historical data are accurate to an extent far surpassing the ideas of any modern critical students, who have consistently tended to err on the side of hypercriticism."[18]

Once again Palestinian archaeology became a tool of theological apologetics. And once again archaeology took up the task of verifying the factual basis of the biblical narrative not only for biblically centered communities but also against other biblical scholars whose methods called into question the ability to claim historical factuality for biblical events. For example, just as earlier Sayce had argued against the "higher" criticism of Wellhausen, beginning in the 1930s Albright battled with the Germans Albrecht Alt and Martin Noth, whose higher literary criticism had made them skeptical about the historicity of the patriarchs.[19] Using archaeological materials, Albright attempted to establish the patriarchs as historical figures who fit into the world of the early second millennium.[20] He concluded that "the patriarchal narratives have a historical nucleus throughout..."[21]

Wright carried this process further by integrating archaeology into an explicit theological framework. This position, which came to be known as biblical theology, placed great importance on the factuality of the major events of the Bible. Because the biblical revelation is identified with specific historical events, one must pay "close attention to the facts of (biblical) history... because these facts are the facts of God."[22] And if God's revelation is to be valid, then the events in the Bible must be actual occurrences. As Wright declared, "Now in Biblical faith everything depends upon whether the central events actually occurred.... [For] to participate in Biblical faith means that we must indeed take history seriously as the primary data of faith."[23] If the facts are centrally important, then establishing their reality provides a basis for trusting the Bible—for faith. For Wright, then, archaeological data became the apologetic foundation for the faith claims of the Bible. Archaeology was the method of demonstrating the factuality of biblical persons and events, making the claim that God had actually worked in these events possible and reasonable. Biblical archaeology was the ground of biblical theology.

It was left to John Bright to write his *A History of Israel* from the perspective of biblical theology. This work instructed generations of seminary students on how archaeology could be correlated with the Bible.[24] Beyond this, Bernhard W. Anderson's widely popular *Understanding the Old Testament*, which relied heavily on the biblical theology movement, did the same for generations of undergraduates.[25] Perhaps this explains why ministers and layfolk who speak about archaeology and the Bible invariably, although unknowingly, do so within the framework of the biblical theology movement.

As we shall see, later archaeologists have criticized this project of the Albright-Wright-Bright school from the vantage point of new archaeological evidence and, methodologically, for having forced the data into a predetermined theological framework. Nevertheless, there are still archaeologists who admit that their secret desire is to substantiate a biblical event for which other archaeologists have found contradictory evidence. For example, Joseph

A. Callaway writes that in 1964, when he arrived at Ai, one of the most problematic biblical sites, he "entertained notions of bridging the widening gulf between the biblical accounts in Joshua 7-8 and the actual evidence of the ruin itself." [26]

The whole discussion thus far has had as its context the archaeology associated with the Hebrew Bible or Old Testament. The reason for this is that until recently Palestinian archaeology meant dealing with sites related to the Hebrew Bible.[27] New Testament archaeology, however, is now an emerging area of studies. In spite of the limitations discovered by those involved in the application of archaeology to the Old Testament, archaeologists involved in the New Testament context have continued to insist on the historical character of the biblical texts and to use archaeological evidence to support the Bible's claims. In their important work *Archaeology, the Rabbis and Early Christianity*, Eric M. Meyers and James F. Strange reject a purely theological interpretation of the New Testament. "Although a theological intent by the various authors of New Testament literature cannot be denied," they write, "it is also true that the New Testament exhibits a historical context or contexts."[28]

Meyers and Strange remain modest in the claims they make for archaeology. For the "historical context" to which archaeology might be applied is the cultural background of the early Christian period. Archaeology can add artifactual data on synagogues, burial customs, roofing methods, and the like. It can contradict or verify historical information referred to in the text.[29] However, it is one thing to claim that writers are grounded in a historical context and therefore reflect actual cultural elements. It is something else to claim that authors produce factually accurate narratives. Meyers and Strange never make the claim—as did the Albright-Wright-Bright school in regard to the Old Testament—that the authors of the gospels had a historical intent or produced historically accurate accounts of Jesus' ministry.

As Meyers and Strange examine the archaeological remains, they make important but cautious conclusions. For instance, in the discussion of the so-called house of Peter in Capernaum, after a review of the archaeological evidence, they affirm the possibility that this structure might have been the house of Peter and therefore the house where Jesus stayed.[30] However, when James Strange joins Hershel Shanks to write an article for the popular *Biblical Archaeology Review*, some of the caution has been left behind and the affirmation is made that this "probably" is the house of Peter.[31]

In his informative and enlightening book, *Jesus Within Judaism*,[32] James Charlesworth brings the results of New Testament archaeology clearly into the lineage of the Albright-Wright-Bright school. This work not only introduces the reader to the amazing archaeological discoveries that can shed light on the New Testament and its Palestinian context, but in it archaeology once again becomes an apologetic strategy, a foundation for establishing the basic historical character of the New Testament texts. Certainly, Charlesworth affirms the kerygmatic intention of the gospel writers, but he is "convinced" that their "historical interest was more considerable than some critics now contend."[33]

Jesus Within Judaism, therefore, time and again takes the reader from archaeological discovery to support for the historical content of a biblical story. Although Charlesworth refrains from claiming certainty, he seems convinced that the house in Capernaum is Peter's house where Jesus stayed.[34] After citing archaeological evidence that this house would have had a roof of "tree branches covered with palm leaves and caked mud," he reminds us of the story of Jesus in the house in Capernaum, healing the paralytic who had been let down through an opening that had been made in the roof. Finally, Charlesworth claims that "thinking on such possibilities" draws us away from ideas about Jesus "to reality and history."[35] When speaking about archaeological discoveries in Jerusalem, Charlesworth several times relates them to passages from the Gospel of John. The discovery of a passageway from the so-called Solomonic Stables to the

Double Gates is tied to John's mention of oxen as well as sheep (John 2:14). The straw and tethers related to large animals are connected to the whip that Jesus made for cleansing the Temple (John 2: 15). The discovery of two pools with a total of five porticoes in the Sheep Gate is related to the pool of Bethesda in John 5:2-9. According to Charlesworth, all of this points to what may be "reliable historical information on Jesus' action in the Temple" preserved in the Gospel of John.[36] Citing evidence that the Church of the Holy Sepulchre is built on the rock where Jesus was crucified and that this rock was part of a rejected quarry, Charlesworth suggests that the biblical passage "The stone which the builders rejected; this has become the head of the corner" (1 Pet. 2:7; Ps. 118:22; cf. Acts 4:11, Mark 12:10) has a double historical referent, Jesus and Golgotha, a rejected quarry stone.[37]

At the end of his chapter on archaeological discoveries, Charlesworth suggests that the announcement of the failure of Albright's synthesis was premature. He concludes with a statement that echoes Albright and Wright and that shows clearly the apologetic position of archaeology:

> As incredible as it once may have sounded, archaeologists are not throwing up debris in the way of Christian faith. In terms of New Testament history they are exposing the arena and bedrock on which faith is founded.[38]

This discussion has attempted to demonstrate how a biblically generated religious imagination has produced the archaeological project in Palestine. Archaeologists, in turn, have used their results to produce interpretations that verify the general historical framework or content of the Bible. They have employed archaeology apologetically as a foundation for the reliability of the biblical narratives and for the possibility of faith. In this case, while there were minor problems, no real contradictions existed between the Bible and archaeology, between faith and history. The rock of the biblical claim and the hard place of the archaeological dig fused together to form the foundation of faith.

THE FAILURE OF ARCHAEOLOGY AS
AN APOLOGETIC STRATEGY

It is not difficult to understand the enthusiasm of archaeologists. Their tedious work has produced astonishing results that are engaging in themselves. The connection of these results with the Bible and biblical context gives them an even greater significance for Jews and Christians. One remarkable type of archaeological discovery has been the unearthing of thousands of ancient written texts on clay tablets, monuments, ostraca, parchments, and papyri. Much of the epigraphic material has come from outside of Palestine, from Mesopotamia and Egypt for instance, but has shed light on biblical customs, background and events, as well as allowing the comparison of biblical narratives with stories from neighboring cultures. Without the Babylonian and Assyrian texts or the Nuzi, Mari, Amarna, Ugaritic and, more recently, Eblaite documents, our understanding of the Old Testament would not be as rich. Without the Dead Sea Scrolls and the Nag Hammadi codices, the same would be true of our comprehension of the New Testament and early Christianity.[39]

The other major type of archaeological evidence is artifactual material. Here the results have been no less significant, for archaeologists can discover the material culture of ancient people—their architecture and technology, the kind of houses they lived in, the type of pottery and tools they used, and how they buried the dead, for example. In this way, archaeologists can draw conclusions about the manner of lives these ancient people had and can compare how life changed in the same location over time, or how one location is related to other locations at the same time. Archaeologists can also determine when a city was first occupied, if and when it was destroyed, and if and when it was rebuilt, thereby gaining clues to a particular site's history. Many of the sites related to cities and villages mentioned in the Hebrew Bible and the New Testament have been examined archaeologically. In fact, according to William Dever, it was in the 1960s that archaeology in Palestine "came of age" and produced a "proliferation of excavations."[40]

It is precisely here, however, that the synthesis between archaeology and the Bible propounded by the Albright school becomes problematic. For the vast increase of new archaeological evidence, added to a continued examination of the method of using archaeology in historical reconstruction and the ongoing literary criticism of the biblical narrative itself, has often driven a wedge between the claims of the Bible and historical factuality. What was earlier interpreted as evidence supporting the historicity of the Bible is reappraised and now challenges the Bible. Continuing archaeological excavation has found no trace of some biblical events and has contradicted others. The attempt to use archaeological artifacts as an apologetic foundation for the Bible has failed. As David N. Freedman declared, "Albright's great plan and expectation to set the Bible firmly on the foundation of archaeology buttressed by verifiable data seems to have foundered.... The Albrightian synthesis has become unglued."[41]

In terms of methodology, J. Maxwell Miller has demonstrated the difficulty in using archaeology in historical reconstruction. He has, in a variety of contexts, exposed the circular reasoning that is frequently operative in such attempts. The archaeological remains usually do not clearly identify the site. The stones remain silent.[42] The archaeologist, therefore, uses the Bible as a means of knowing which ancient city is being excavated. Then in interpreting the artifacts, it is again the Bible that provides the framework for relating ancient constructions and destructions to particular times and people. If the evidence is ambiguous or does not in fact fit the working model, the archaeologist offers interpretations to resolve the difficulties and align the evidence with the biblical information. After having done all of this, the archaeologist claims that the excavation has supported the biblical account.[43] What has in fact occurred is that the Bible has interpreted the archaeologist's data. It is therefore improper "to cite the interpreted archaeological data in turn as 'proof' of the accuracy of the written source."[44] This means that many of the earlier correlations between archaeology and the Bible were the products of faulty methodology and gratuitous interpretation.

Nevertheless, it is not the critique of method but the increase in archaeological data that has resulted in the collapse of the synthesis between archaeology and the Bible and led a retreat away from claiming historicity for many biblical events. This retreat was already seen in Albright and Wright, for they both knew that archaeology contradicted many aspects of the biblical story.[45] Yet now archaeological data are calling into question the historical character of major biblical events. In fact, archaeology has not been able to support the historicity of a single major event in the Pentateuch. On the contrary, it has provided some of the basis to think otherwise.

Modern science had already criticized the literal understanding of the creation stories.[46] But archaeology added its part as well. For in light of the recovery of ancient Mesopotamian texts, it is evident that many elements of Genesis 1 are borrowed from the Babylonian creation story (*Enuma Elish*) while images in Genesis 2 appeared first in the Gilgamesh Epic. The biblical flood story has likewise received an archaeological critique. While archaeologists have found evidence of inundations in lower Mesopotamia, there is no archaeological foundation for a belief in a universal flood. Furthermore, the story of Noah's Ark has features so strikingly similar to Utnapishtim's flood story in the Epic of Gilgamesh that the biblical writers must have used material from the earlier Babylonian account.[47] In fact, the whole structure of the story that begins with the creation of humans and runs through the threat of human annihilation by flood might well be borrowed from the even older Babylonian flood story Atrahasis.[48]

It is not only to the critique of the Bible's primeval history, however, that archaeology offers material. Archaeology also fails to support the patriarchal and exodus traditions. Many scholars, including Max Miller, generally accept Thomas L. Thompson's assessment of the patriarchal narratives. After an exhaustive treatment of the archaeological evidence, Thompson states that, "it must be concluded that any such historicity as is commonly spoken of in both scholarly and popular works about the Patriarchs of Genesis is hardly possible and totally improbable."[49] Max Miller points to the inability to draw conclusions about the patriarchs from archaeology because, even with the Nuzi, Mari, Amarna and Ebla material, "the Bible remains our only primary ancient source which actually mentions, or even alludes to, the Hebrew patriarchs."[50] The same type of conclusions have been reached about the exodus traditions. Again, Thomas Thompson surveys the archaeological data and the attempted correlations. After adding to this a review of how the Joseph and Moses material have story after story that are typical of ancient Near Eastern literature, he concludes that "not only is their historical relevance and accuracy unattested, but their literary genre is essentially ahistorical...and fundamentally disruptive to historical categories." "Nothing more historically concrete about the historical Moses and Yahweh can be known than can be known about the historical Tammuz and Ishtar...."[51]

In their recent book, *A History of Ancient Israel and Judah*, Max Miller and his Emory University colleague John H. Hayes show the effect of recent archaeology as well as literary studies on the writing of a history of Palestine. After discussing the relevant issues relating to Israel's early history, they defer any correlations with archaeology and "decline any attempt to reconstruct the earliest history of Israel."[52] That is, they produce a history of Israel without reference to the patriarchs or, even more astounding, without reference to Moses and the exodus.

They begin their historical reconstruction only with the rise of Israel in Canaan. And yet some scholars still believe they say too much. This has resulted in Max Miller producing a defense of writing any history of ancient Israel for members of the Society of Biblical Literature.[53]

Even when beginning a history of Israel with Israel's appearance in Canaan, archaeology does not support the biblical record or the correlations made by Albright, Wright, and Bright. These biblical traditions as well have fallen under the weight of archaeological evidence and interpretive critique. The well-known sites of Jericho and Ai are cases in point. These cities which, according to the Bible, the invading Israelites under Joshua destroyed, archaeologists tell us were actually uninhabited at the time.[54] In light of all the archaeological evidence, Miller claims that the invasion theory of the settlement of Israel in Canaan—the view supported by the Book of Joshua—has collapsed.[55] "Were we dependent upon archaeological and other nonbiblical evidence alone," Miller writes, "we would have no reason even to suppose that such a conquest ever occurred."[56] Rather, the view now current is that the Israelite tribes "emerged gradually and naturally in Palestine from the indigenous population."[57] Once again archaeology fails to support the biblical history.

Furthermore, when correlations between biblical events and persons and artifactual remains become possible—perhaps beginning with David and Solomon—the problems do not end. For David and Solomon are not mentioned in a single ancient extrabiblical source that has yet been unearthed. In terms of artifactual evidence in Jerusalem, their capital city, J. Alberto Soggin claims that Wright's statement is still true: "Not a single discovery has been made in Jerusalem which can be dated with any certainty to the time of David and Solomon."[58] Structures in other cities (Megiddo, Hazor, and Gezer) that have been associated with Solomon's reign, while impressive, are "rather ordinary when compared" with others, even those of Omri and Ahab in the same cities. As Miller concludes about Solomon: "He is probably the most overrated monarch in all of history."[59] The glorious kingdom of the biblical story's two greatest kings turns out to have been rather modest, according to archaeological evidence and historical analysis.[60]

On the other hand, the ninth-century king Omri had accomplishments that were substantial. He and his son Ahab are the first biblical figures mentioned in sources outside the Bible. The Moabite Stone claims that Omri subjugated Moab, and Assyrian records call Palestine the "land of Omri" a hundred years after his reign. The excavations of Samaria, built by Omri as a new capital, and other cities have demonstrated impressive structures built by him and Ahab. Yet the biblical narrative devotes only eight verses to Omri (1 Kings 17: 21-28) and condemns him as it later does Ahab. The Bible, therefore, emphasizes and glorifies the more modest reigns of David and Solomon, about whom no foreign nations ever spoke. At the same time, the Bible deprecates and suppresses the reigns of two impressive kings who are seen as prestigious in the records of ancient foreign powers. Again, far from acting as an apologetic support for the veracity of the Bible, archaeology has challenged the historicity of the biblical story.

If archaeological data have failed to support the historical claims of the Old Testament, perhaps they will serve the New Testament better. The New Testament texts and the events to which it points are, after all, closer to us in time. If archaeology cannot serve as the apologetic foundation for the Hebrew Bible, perhaps it can for the New Testament. As I argued earlier, this is the direction in which James Charlesworth is moving, emphasizing the historical concern of the New Testament writers and therefore our ability to see what Jesus was really like more clearly by appealing to the results of archaeological work (both texts and artifacts). Because of the relative youth of the New Testament archaeological enterprise, there does not yet exist a great body of archaeological and New Testament syntheses followed by the inevitable critiques. Nevertheless, for several reasons, I believe that the attempt at synthesis that Charlesworth makes in *Jesus Within Judaism* will be subjected to the same type of critique that has been leveled against the Albright-Wright-Bright school. First, some of the archaeological evidence to which Charlesworth gives a positive interpretation has been interpreted very differently by other scholars. For instance, consider the question of the origin of the synagogue, which has long been a historical problem.[61]

Until recently, there has been little archaeological evidence for the existence of pre-70 C.E. synagogues in Palestine. The claims of the New Testament that Jesus taught in the synagogues were, therefore, seen as an anachronistic reading of later developments back into the story.[62] Charlesworth, however, points to three examples of pre-70 synagogues in Palestine at Masada, the Herodium, and Gamla. He also cites the Theodotus inscription, which honors Theodotus for having built a synagogue in Jerusalem, as pre-70 evidence. He recognizes that these "synagogues" were not specific architectural styles, but usually merely rooms in other structures. Nevertheless, he identifies them as synagogues.[63] On this basis, he calls attention to the New Testament references to Jesus teaching in the synagogues and urges the reader "to think historically and sociologically" about the meaning of Jesus' synagogue activity. Charlesworth correlates the archaeological evidence with the biblical events and believes that in this way "we are brought closer to the tradition of Jesus'" activity in relation to the synagogue.[64]

Other scholars, on the other hand, give different interpretations to this same archaeological evidence. Howard Clark Kee refuses to identify private houses where people gathered for prayer as synagogues.[65] This means that for him Gamla and Magdala are not synagogues. In this interpretation, Kee is joined by Joseph Gutman.[66] They both also reject the claim that the rooms at Herodium and Masada were synagogues. They were "nothing more than rooms that had been used for meetings."[67] As Gutman declares, "There is no proof of piety or of a definite place of worship other than the (excavator's) wishful thinking."[68] On the Theodotus inscription, Kee agrees with archaeologists who date it to 125-150 C.E. [69] One does not have to take sides in this debate in order to perceive the tenuous nature of supporting the historicity of certain features of the New Testament on archaeological grounds. The archaeologists themselves cannot agree on the interpretation of the artifacts.

Nevertheless, it is not only on details such as the synagogue that Charlesworth might be challenged, but on some of the central aspects of the portrait of Jesus that he draws. Charlesworth develops a picture of Jesus that in many features is familiar (and with which I tend to agree). For instance, the apocalyptic component of Jesus' preaching is affirmed. The kingdom of God is the center of this preaching.[70] Jesus remains firmly rooted in Judaism. He does not employ "Greek paradigms and linguistic models,"[71] and he directs his ministry not to gentiles but only to Israel.[72]

This image of Jesus, however, is increasingly being attacked, and precisely by New Testament scholars who, in addition to literary study of the gospels, are taking archaeological research seriously. One major influence in the recent reevaluation of Jesus is the excavation being done by James Strange and Eric Meyers at Sepphoris, a major Hellenistic city close to Nazareth. Howard Clark Kee suggests that Jesus and/or his father might have worked as builders (*tektontes*) there. More importantly, Kee stresses the possible Hellenistic influence on Jesus, that he was most likely bilingual and taught in gentile areas.[73] In his recent challenging book, *A Myth of Innocence*, Burton L. Mack also highlights the influence of Hellenistic culture on Jesus. He presents a non-apocalyptic Jesus and claims that the kingdom of God sayings need not be given an apocalyptic interpretation. Instead, Mack stresses the authenticity of the aphoristic sayings and sees the Hellenistic cynic teacher as the best model for understanding Jesus.[74]

Once again, one does not have to decide about this debate to comprehend the issue. Archaeology has not served as a basis to bring agreement about the historical Jesus or the historicity of the New Testament. Charlesworth claims that the New Testament presents a recognizable portrait of Jesus.[75] Burton Mack claims that there is "at the moment no firm consensus about Jesus (or) the nature of his activity...."[76] Charlesworth argues for the historical intent of the New Testament writers.[77] Mack stresses, for instance, that "Mark's story is most probably Mark's fiction."[78] Archaeology, in spite of its vast gifts to New Testament research, has so far failed, as it did in relation to the Hebrew Bible before, to provide an apologetic basis for the veracity of the historical component in the New Testament.

This analysis has shown that the archaeological project in Palestine has not done what the earlier archaeologists hoped it would. Far from establishing the apologetic basis to support the historicity of biblical claims and the faith, it has challenged this historicity. Archaeology has added its impetus for modern scholarship's continuous retreat from the assumption of the factuality of biblical events. Archaeology has turned on its own source—the biblically inspired religious imagination—to masticate it between the rock of the biblical narrative and the hard place of archaeological contradiction.

The results of the excavation of Palestine raise again the question of the authenticity of the Bible and the object of faith. What is faith to trust when not just this fact or that one is shown to be inaccurate, but when major, fundamental events of the biblical story are challenged? Perhaps faith can stand without a historical Adam and Eve or flood, and perhaps without Abraham and Sarah, Isaac and Rebekah, and Jacob and his wives. But what does faith trust without an exodus event or when the achievements of David and Solomon were modest when compared to those of Omri and Ahab? Where is faith grounded when archaeology only complicates further an attempt to find the Jesus of history? The negative results of archaeological research raise the question of the nature of faith and its relation to history to a higher key.

TOWARD AN ARCHAEOLOGY OF FAITH

A variety of responses is available to this issue raised for faith by archaeology. Two options attempt to alleviate the tension caused by the clash between the Bible and archaeology by eliminating one of them. One response might be to reject the archaeological results that question the historical accuracy of the Bible. This response, which is associated with fundamentalism and what we might call the "Jerry Falwell" answer, claims that the Bible is accurate in every detail and therefore there must be something mistaken in the archaeological conclusions.[79] Of course, this option allows one to select those archaeological items that are believed still to hold the possibility of verifying the Bible. This explains the regular appearance in the popular press of references to excursions to Mount Ararat in search of Noah's Ark and the recent excitement in the churches when the popular press announced that Bryant Wood's analysis of the excavation of Jericho had confirmed the Bible.[80] On the other hand is the response that accepts the archaeological results and rejects the Bible. We might call this option the "Carl Sagan" approach.[81] In this case, if the facts of the Bible are inaccurate, then the Bible is useless and must be abandoned in favor of a factually accurate account.

Actually, both of these options have a common base—the equation of truth with factuality. Both are generated by the modern scientific, positivistic mentality. For each it is the facts that are determinative; thus, in order to have faith in the Bible, it must contain correct, verifiable information. On this basis Falwellians would reject archaeology in the name of the factuality of the Bible while Saganites would reject the Bible in the name of the factuality of archaeology. In truth, Falwellians and Saganites are blood brothers. Both tend to turn faith into a matter of assent to facts; one accepts the facts of faith, the other does not.

This understanding of faith, however, which is grounded on factuality, must be negated. It is a faith that tends to reduce the Bible to a repository of information which, if it is to be accepted, must close its eyes to historical research. It maintains belief in its facts only by sealing itself off from the world, including the results of archaeology. In reality, this type of faith is a modern invention that is true neither to the biblical message nor the Christian tradition.

Another way of responding to the questions posed to faith by archaeological research might be found in the early church. An examination of early Christian theology reveals that we are not the first community committed to the Bible that has had to struggle with faith in light of places in which the Bible appears unbelievable. The early church fathers confronted this issue already. Certainly, they believed that most of the stories were factually true, and the worldview that the Bible expresses they took as self evident. Nevertheless, on the one hand, they did not limit the meaning of the text which was believed factually to the literal level. On the other hand, if a passage could not be believed on the literal level, they sought for deeper meaning. In both cases they employed typological and allegorical interpretations to expose the spiritual meaning of the text.

While the use of allegory appeared earlier in Judaism with Philo and in Christianity in the Epistle of Barnabas, Clement, and Origen,[82] Augustine can serve as an example of this approach. Augustine, who had been trained in rhetoric, had difficulty making sense out of the "ancient scriptures." In his *Confessions* he writes that his literal understanding of the texts had "made them seem absurd" and that he had criticized the "saints for holding beliefs which they had never really held at all." He learned from Ambrose of Milan to find "the spiritual meaning of texts which, taken literally, appeared to contain the most unlikely doctrines."[83] In *On Christian Doctrine*, the most influential work on biblical exposition during the Middle Ages,[84] Augustine develops his understanding of allegorical interpretation. He does not ignore the historical nature of the biblical books. Frequently, he raises issues of authorship and the dating of the books and discusses the author's intended meaning.[85] Nevertheless, even if the text were from his perspective literally correct, allegory could show its deeper, spiritual significance. The flood, for instance, is allegorically interpreted as Jesus' action on behalf of the future church. Those on the ark are the church, the ark itself, the cross and the flood, the "submersion of this world."[86] Furthermore, when a text held an "unlikely doctrine," which Augustine could not accept literally, allegory allowed him still to find meaning in it. Thus if biblical heroes acted immorally or wickedly in a way that could not be rationalized, then these texts were seen as "wholly figurative."[87]

Allegory certainly is not an adequate means of biblical interpretation. However, the point is clear that throughout most of its history the church had a means of dealing with biblical passages that were considered historically problematic. A spiritual meaning was still available. Furthermore, even if the event were historically accepted, its meaning was not exhausted in its historicity. Faith in the biblical claim was not a matter of mere factuality. Faith had room for human knowledge derived from other sources. In this sense, the allegorical method, though ancient, is an advance beyond the Falwellian approach.

Nevertheless, allegorical interpretation must be criticized. For such a system, in which the beautiful woman in the "Song of Songs" is the church and where, in the parable of the Good Samaritan, the man going down from Jerusalem to Jericho is Adam falling from paradise to death and "the thieves are the devil and his angels,"[88] turns out to be speculative and ahistorical. Allegory lends itself to an interpretation which is completely detached from the historical or contextual meaning of a passage. A danger here, then, is that faith might find its ground in speculation, losing its basis in the biblical claim of God's work in history.

A faith that is grounded in the biblical witness, however, cannot escape history either through a denial of historical data (i.e., the Falwellian option) or through allegorical flights of imagination. As we demonstrated earlier, one of the

central themes of the Bible is that God works in the history
of ancient Israel and becomes incarnate in Jesus. Biblical faith
is constituted in response to an encounter with this God who
is active in history. If we wish to remain in this faith without
closing our eyes to other areas of knowledge, we must find
an understanding of God's work in history that allows us at
the same time to accept the results of archaeology, as well as
other human disciplines. That is, like Augustine, we need an
understanding that allows the Bible to speak both when it is
and when it is not historically accurate. The basis of this
understanding, I believe, is the event of God's incarnation in
Jesus. If it is the perception of the incarnational God that gives
rise to archaeology in the first place, then understanding the
incarnation more profoundly might offer responses to the
questions addressed to faith by archaeology.

The biblical theology movement, championed by Wright,
was correct in its perception that the biblical God was a God
who acts in history. The problem with this movement was
that its understanding of God's work in history did not
penetrate deeply enough. Biblical theology tended to focus
upon the great acts of God in the biblical narrative, thereby
giving the impression that God's activity in history was
merely episodic and related to the miraculous.[89] For the
Christian faith, however, God's action in history is primarily
seen in and defined by the incarnation, God's becoming
human in Jesus. While the biblical writers speak of miracles
accompanying this event, they make it clear that the
miraculous does not prove or constitute it and that faith
grounded merely in miracles is inadequate. Rather, the
central and deepest point of the incarnational event is the
cross. That is, the greatest act of God in history is where there
is not what is usually thought of as a great act, precisely
where there is no miracle, no supernatural intervention. Here
God acts by identifying with human history completely.
Here God works in complete identity with a human being,
and with this human being God and God's work are subject
to all the ambiguities, accidents, limitations, developments,

and terrors of history. The early church from New Testament times through the trinitarian and christological controversies rejected every attempt—whether from Arian, docetic, or ebionite tendencies—to deny or limit God's authentic identification with human history in Jesus.

If God's work in history must be understood more deeply in light of the incarnation, it must be understood more broadly as well. God's incarnation in Jesus is not a closed event. For it reveals the way in which God has always acted and continues to act in and through history. This incarnational event is open towards the past as it perceives God's work in and identification with ancient Israel as narrated in the Hebrew Bible, not merely in the so-called great acts but primarily in God's indwelling with the people. This incarnational event is open towards the future as well. God continues to work in the Spirit in history. Because this Spirit is also the God who is defined by the incarnation event, here God acts in the same way, not destroying but acting under the conditions of history, even in and through the, at times, terrifying history of the church.

The consequences of this incarnational understanding of God's work in history for our discussion on the relationship of the Bible, archaeology, and faith are significant and varied. First, the openness of God's incarnational event means that the biblical authors and editors, as well as those involved in the process of canonization, can be understood not merely as witnessing to the work of God in history but as part of the history of God's work. God is working in and through these writers and canonizers, but in the manner revealed in the history of Jesus, that is, in and through their human history with all its limitations. As these authors worked to proclaim the activity of God in their history, God was at work establishing their message as authentic, not miraculously and "divinely" overcoming their historical human context, but in and through it. This means that as the biblical writers worked, their imaginations operated as human beings of particular times and places. If they used legends, tribal sagas, folk stories, cultic material, Babylonian myths, Mesopotamian legal codes, etiologies, miracle stories, and Hellenistic concepts that were common at various times, or even if they created imaginative stories which they portrayed as historical events, an incarnational perspective would find no reason for surprise. This does not destroy the truth claim of the Bible. For even if there were no historical exodus, for instance, its assertion that God has worked in the history of the Israelites and formed them into a people remains, however it may have factually occurred. There is no threat, therefore, to the truthfulness of the Bible or to the possibility of faith should archaeologists find no trace of some biblical stories, or find some material borrowed from earlier cultures or find evidence that contradicts the biblical presentation. On the contrary, such findings can be viewed as testimony to the incarnational way in which God works. They do not eliminate God from history, but rather demonstrate how deeply God has identified with it.

The second result of the incarnational approach is faith's freedom for archaeology. Hugh Anderson is correct, as Charlesworth notes, to claim that it is not "theologically unjustifiable...to seek for historical knowledge."[90] Indeed, an incarnationally grounded faith not only allows historical research, but compels it. Such a faith continues to claim that God has worked in the history of certain people in certain times and in the recording of their history with God. Faith must be interested in those places and times so that it can better understand the events that did take place and also the contexts in which the biblical authors wrote. Furthermore, archaeological and historical work can keep the faithful honest; it can keep their eyes open. The data from an excavation, for instance, can prevent us from emphasizing as factual biblical accounts that are improbable at best. To accomplish these tasks, faith must declare archaeology free to follow its own methods and draw its conclusions according to its own canon. In doing this, archaeology can be a work of love in the service of faith's quest for understanding.

However, the third result of an incarnational perspective is the recognition of faith's freedom from archaeology, that is, the recognition of the strict limits of archaeology. Archaeology can serve faith, but it cannot produce or serve as an apologetic ground for faith. An irony in the quest for the historicity of the biblical events and the quest for the Jesus of history is that even if archaeology could verify the entire Bible as factually accurate or verify a particular portrait of Jesus so that we could know what he thought and what he said and when he said it, this would not produce faith. Archaeologists cannot dig up the incarnation or the resurrected Jesus. Archaeology can excavate the land and find artifacts of the history in which God has been active, but it cannot dig up the evidence that God has indeed been active there. In the depth and breadth of the incarnational event, God is so closely identified with human history that the divine work is never merely obvious. It is always open to trivial interpretation and can be perceived only in the response of faith.

This was the mistake of the eighteenth-century thinker, Gotthold Lessing, who despaired over the "ugly, broad ditch" of history that separated him from the time of Jesus. He believed that seeing the facts themselves was the basis of faith and thus asserted that if he had only seen Jesus fulfill prophecies and perform miracles that he "would willingly have believed him in all things."[91] In the next century, Søren Kierkegaard responded that an original disciple of Jesus had no advantage in terms of faith.[92] We must take Kierkegaard's claim even further and assert that the original disciples had a clear disadvantage. They had no long tradition of a faith response to God's appearance in Jesus. They could not romanticize or idealize him for, if the incarnational view presented here is correct, when they saw him it was no supernatural, spiritual being they experienced, but a fully human person who had to eat and sleep, who sweated and got dirty, and who finally was executed on a cross. In light of these facts of history, for these disciples to claim later that they had encountered this man as the living Christ, the Son of God, took a profound response of faith. This faith is not grounded in the mere facts of history. Indeed, this faith has no ground except, with eyes open to all the ambiguities, the response made possible by the ongoing incarnational work of God. This is why most people in the first century who encountered Jesus or preaching about him did not become Christians.

Consequently, another limit of archaeology is reached. Archaeological data cannot only not produce faith but they cannot, as some archaeologists suggest, be used to distinguish among the competing claims made by groups who want to interpret Jesus as supporting their position.[93] Archaeological and historical presentations of Jesus, as helpful and compelling as they might be, can never in themselves be normative for faith. Archaeological investigation may or may not be able to show us the Jesus of history more clearly. But if it can, then we find ourselves in the position of Kierkegaard's original disciple. The question becomes, What do we do with these facts? From the perspective of the depth and breath of God's incarnational work, the basis of the Christian faith is God's activity in Jesus; but it is that activity as interpreted by the early Christians, the biblical writers, and the church as it formed the canon. For this tradition as well, canonized in the text of the Bible, is included in God's incarnational activity. The archaeological and historical data do not hold the key for a correct interpretation of faith; the biblical writers had that already.

CONCLUSION

Faith in the God who works in history generates the archaeological quest to support the biblical claims. Because of the archaeological contradiction of many biblical accounts, we find ourselves between a rock and a hard place, between the claims of faith and the facts of history. This forces us back to a reconsideration of the meaning of incarnation and the foundation of faith. What we discover is that the discontinuity between the Bible and archaeology, faith and history, is actually the result of the incarnational event itself, the result of the way in which God identifies with and works through ordinary history. This means, on the one hand, that some of the content of the Bible might be the product of the human imagination and not factual at all. On the other hand, even if archaeology can verify the biblical events, there is no verification of the incarnational work of God. Therefore we remain between a rock and a hard place in spite of our desire for certainty. For God, by entering human history, calls us into an arena of open questions that is the crisis of all systems that claim certainty. As Flannery O'Connor's Misfit declared, "Jesus thrown everything off balance."[94] It is precisely faith in the incarnation of God that places us and keeps us between a rock and a hard place, because it is precisely there that God has chosen to work and be.

NOTES

1. See James P. Mackey, *Modern Theology: A Sense of Direction* (New York: Oxford University Press, 1987), 1ff., where he claims that the relationship between faith and history is one of the three major questions of modern theology. According to Mackey, another of the major issues—one which is a specific example of the first and is relevant for our topic—is the question of the historical Jesus.

2. Jonathan Z. Smith, "Narratives Into Problems: The College Introductory Course and the Study of Religion," *Journal of the American Academy of Religion* 56/4 (Winter 1988): 736.

3. The literature on this hymn is voluminous. An excellent treatment is Ernst Käsemann, "A Critical Analysis of Philippians 2: 5-11," trans. Alice F. Carse, *Journal for Theology and the Church* 5 (1968): 45-88. On its pre-Pauline character, see, for instance, Günther Bornkamm, "On Understanding the Christ Hymn," *Early Christian Experience* (London: SCM Press, 1969), 113ff.

4. On this, see Rowan Williams, *Christian Spirituality* (Atlanta: John Knox, 1980), 48.

5. For an analysis of this, see Jürgen Moltmann, *The Trinity and the Kingdom* (San Francisco: Harper & Row, 1981), 23ff.

6. Ibid., 28. Moltmann here draws upon rabbinic sources as he analyzes the concept of Shekinah (see 25-30).

7. See George E. Mendenhall, "Biblical Interpretation and the Albright School" in Leo G. Perdue, Lawrence E. Toombs and Gary Lance Johnson, eds., *Archaeology and Biblical Interpretation* (Atlanta: John Knox Press, 1987), 5. Mendenhall is paraphrasing William Dever's description. See Dever's section on "The Patriarchal Traditions" in John H. Hayes and J. Maxwell Miller, eds., *Israelite and Judean History* (Philadelphia: Westminster Press, 1977), 74. Hereafter cited as *IJH*.

8. William F. Albright, *The Archeology of Palestine* (Baltimore: Penguin Books, 1949), 219.

9. G. Ernest Wright, "The Present State of Biblical Archaeology" (1947), quoted by William Dever, "Syro-Palestinian and Biblical Archaeology," in Douglas A. Knight and Gene M. Tucker, eds., *The Hebrew Bible and Its Modern Interpreters* (Chico, Calif.: Scholars Press, 1985), 55. Hereafter cited as *HBMI*. See also the statement of Joseph A. Callaway in "Ai (Et-Tell): Problem site or Biblical Archaeologists" in Perdue, Toombs, and Johnson, *Archaeology*, 97: "One function of archaeological research is to redirect our thinking about the Bible."

10. Philip J. King, *American Archaeology in the Mideast: A History of the American Schools of Oriental Research* (Philadelphia: The American Schools of Oriental Research, 1983), 2.

11. Ibid.

12. In Perdue, Toombs, and Johnson, *Archaeology*, 35ff. Stern also cites his teacher Nahman Avigad from his publication of the bullae of Berechia and Jerahmeel as an example of the relationship between archaeology and the Bible. Avigad wrote: "In conclusion I cannot abstain from expressing my own feelings when handling and deciphering these two bullae for the first time. One has the feeling of personal contact with persons who figure prominently in the dramatic events in which the giant figure of Jeremiah and his faithful follower Baruch were involved at a most critical time preceding the downfall of Judah"(36).

13. See King, *American Archaeology*, 13ff.

14. Quoted in ibid., 14, from Archibald H. Sayce, *The "Higher Criticism" and the Verdict of the Monuments* (London: 1894), 554. In 1924, Ernst Sellin, in "Archeology versus Wellhausenism," expressed the

conviction that in light of archaeological work the era of Wellhausen and higher criticism was "antiquated and wholly of the past" (see King, *American Archaeology*, 15). In the first decades of this century, Melvin Kyle produced a series of books such as *The Deciding Voice of the Monuments in Biblical Criticism*, in which he used archaeological evidence to attempt to prove the historical veracity of the Pentateuch, including its Mosaic authorship. On this, see King, *American Archaeology*, 82ff.

15. Ibid., 15ff. George A. Barton, responding to Melvin Kyle (see n. 14), also warned that one should "not blindly accept" the results of archaeology in support of the factuality of biblical events (ibid., 83).

16. Quoted in ibid., 25.

17. G. Ernest Wright, *God Who Acts: Biblical Theology as Recital* (London: SCM Press, 1952), 127.

18. Albright, *Archaeology of Palestine*, 229.

19. See Dever, "Syro-Palestinian and Biblical Archeology," *HBMI*, 55f. See also J. Maxwell Miller, "Israelite History," *HBMI*, 19ff.

20. See Albright, *Archaeology of Palestine*, 83-98.

21. Ibid., 236.

22. Wright, *God Who Acts*, 38.

23. Ibid., 126f.

24. John Bright, *A History of Israel* (Philadelphia: Westminster Press, 1959, 1972).

25. Bernhard W. Anderson, *Understanding the Old Testament* (Englewood Cliffs, N.J.: Prentice-Hall, 1946, 1952, 1971, 1984). In his 1984 edition, Anderson has moved away somewhat from the perspective of biblical theology.

26. Callaway, "Ai," 90.

27. On this, see Eric M. Meyers and James F. Strange, *Archaeology, the Rabbis, and Early Christianity* (Nashville: Abingdon Press, 1981), 19ff.: "The rubric "archaeology of the New Testament" or even "New Testament archaeology" is not normally recognized as a specialization within the wider discipline of New Testament scholarship, even though the parallel phenomenon in Old Testament studies has a long and honorable history" (23). That this is the case is seen in the fact that unlike its companion volume, *HBMI, The New Testament and Its Modern Interpreters*, eds. Eldon Jay Epp and George W. MacRae (Atlanta: Scholars Press, 1989), has no section dealing with the New Testament and archaeology.

28. Meyers and Strange, *Archaeology, Rabbis, Christianity*, 23.

29. Ibid., 28ff.

30. Ibid., 26, 128-30.

31. James F. Strange and Hershel Shanks, "Has the House Where Jesus Stayed in Capernaum Been Found?" *Biblical Archeology Review* 8 (1982): 26-37. See particularly pages 26 and 30.

32. James H. Charlesworth, *Jesus Within Judaism: New Light from Exciting Archaeological Discoveries* (New York: Doubleday, 1988).

33. Ibid., 13.

34. Ibid., 109-15.

35. Ibid., 112.

36. Ibid., 117-20.

37. Ibid., 124.

38. Ibid., 127.

39. On texts relevant for Old Testament study, see James B. Pritchard, *Archaeology and the Old Testament* (Princeton: Princeton University Press, 1958); J. Maxwell Miller, *The Old Testament and the Historian* (Philadelphia: Fortress Press, 1976), 4-11; H. Darrell Lance, *The Old Testament and the Archaeologist* (Philadelphia: Fortress Press, 1981), 1-10. For New Testament study, see Charlesworth, *Jesus Within Judaism*, 54-102.

40. See Dever, "Syro-Palestinian and Biblical Archeology," *HBMI*, 36-38, for a listing of major excavations between 1960 and 1970.

41. Quoted in Charlesworth, *Jesus Within Judaism*, 126.

42. See J. Maxwell Miller, "New Directions in the Study of Israelite History," *Ned. Geref. Teologiese Tydskrif*, 153.

43. See Miller, *Old Testament and the Historian*, 43-48, where he demonstrates this method and problem in regards to the excavation of Sabaste.

44. Ibid., 47.

45. See Albright, *Archaeology of Palestine*, 236ff, and Wright, *God Who Acts*, 127ff.

46. The recognition that the creation stories cannot be read in a literal fashion is not only modern. Origen (b. 186 C.E.) already asked how "evening and morning existed without the sun…" and claimed that Genesis 1-3 was full of "figurative expressions" (*First Principles* 4.3.1). See also Augustine, *City of God* 9.7.

47. For a popular review of the "Noah's Ark" controversy, see Lloyd R. Bailey, *Where is Noah's Ark?* (Nashville: Abingdon Press, 1978).

48. On this, see Norman K. Gottwald, *The Hebrew Bible: A Socio-Literary Introduction* (Philadelphia: Fortress Press, 1985), 332f. See also Lance, *Old Testament and Archaeologist*, 5f.

49. Thomas L. Thompson, *The Historicity of the Patriarchal Narratives: The Quest for the Historical Abraham* (Berlin: Giessen, 1974), 328; quoted in Hayes and Miller, *IJH*, 98. On Miller's acceptance of Thompson, see Miller, "New Directions," 156.

50. Miller, "Israelite History," *HBMI*, 10.

51. Hayes and Miller, *IJH*, 212, 177.

52. J. Maxwell Miller and John H. Hayes, *A History of Ancient Israel and Judah* (Philadelphia: Westminster Press, 1986), 79.

53. See J. Maxwell Miller, "In Defense of Writing a History of Israel," *Journal for the Study of the Old Testament* 39 (1987): 53-57.

54. See Callaway on "Ai." Recently Bryant G. Wood, "Did the Israelites Conquer Jericho?" *Biblical Archeology Review* 16 (March 1990): 45-57, has reevaluated Kathleen Kenyon's excavational data and argued for a 1400 B.C.E. date for the destruction of Jericho. He then correlates the data with the biblical narrative in an attempt to support

an Israelite conquest. He does not, however, give God the credit for the collapse of the walls, but credits an earthquake (56). Furthermore, even if Wood turns out to be correct in his dating, 1400 is earlier by 150 to 200 years than most scholars date the appearance of Israelites in Canaan. Wood is promising another article, however, where he will argue for an earlier date for the exodus. Finally, it must be said that one city, even Jericho, correlating well with the Bible would not be sufficient to support an invasion theory of Israelite settlement.

55. See Miller, "New Directions," 156.

56. Miller, "Israelite History," 11. Except for Merneptah's stele (ca. 1230) that mentions "Israel is laid waste, his seed is not," there is no extrabiblical source that mentions Israel before the ninth century. Miller doubts, however, that without the Bible, historians would have translated this hieroglyphic name as "Israel" (Miller, "Is it Possible to Write a History of Israel Without Relying on the Hebrew Bible?" address to the Society of Biblical Literature, Anaheim, 1989).

57. Miller, "New Directions," 156. See also Miller and Hayes, *History,* 78f.

58. From Hayes and Miller, *IJH,* 341.

59. See Miller, "New Directions," 158.

60. Ibid. See also Miller and Hayes, *History,* 149-216.

61. On this debate about the synagogue, see Joseph Gutmann, comp., *The Synagogue: Studies in Origins, Archaeology and Architecture* (New York: Ktav Publishing House, 1975).

62. On this, see Howard Clark Kee, "The Transformation of the Synagogue After 70 C.E.: Its Import For Early Christianity," *New Testament Studies* 36 (1990): 1-24.

63. See Charlesworth, *Jesus Within Judaism,* 108f.

64. Ibid., 115.

65. Kee, "Transformation of Synagogue," 8.

66. Gutmann, *Synagogue,* 9.

67. Kee, "Transformation of Synagogue," 8.

68. Gutman, *Synagogue,* xi.

69. Kee, "Transformation of Synagogue," 7.

70. Charlesworth, *Jesus Within Judaism,* 38, 135.

71. Ibid., 90.

72. Ibid., 16.

73. Howard Clark Kee, "The Import of Archaeological Investigations in Galilee for Scholarly Reassessment of the Gospels" (address to Archaeology of the New Testament Group of the Society of Biblical Literature, Anaheim, 1989).

74. Burton L. Mack, *A Myth of Innocence* (Philadelphia: Fortress Press), 53-77. The mentioning of Kee and Mack together on this one point does not imply that they agree on the general portrayal of Jesus.

75. Charlesworth, *Jesus Within Judaism,* 21f.

76. Mack, *Myth,* 56.

77. Charlesworth, *Jesus Within Judaism,* 13.

78. Mack, *Myth,* 11.

79. See Jerry Falwell, *Listen America* (New York: Doubleday, 1980), 63: "The Bible is absolutely infallible, without error in all matters pertaining to faith and practice, as well as in areas such as geography, science, history, etc." See also, Jerry Falwell, *The Fundamentalist Phenomenon* (New York: Doubleday, 1981), 8.

80. See n.54.

81. See Carl Sagan, *Cosmos* (New York: Random House, 1980), where he continually criticizes the Judeo-Christian tradition (91, 174f, 176, 188, 184). While much criticism of the tradition is justifiable, Sagan is generally myopic in terms of his understanding of religion.

82. See Justo L. Gonzalez, *A History of Christian Thought*, 3 vols. (Nashville: Abingdon Press, 1970), 1, 42-220.

83. Augustine, *Confessions* 6.4.2.

84. On this, see Edgar V. McKnight, *Postmodern Use of the Bible* (Nashville: Abingdon Press, 1988), 29. The following discussion of Augustine is indebted to McKnight's analysis.

85. See Augustine, *On Christian Doctrine* (*OCD*) 1.36.40; 1.32.41; 2.2.3.

86. See McKnight, *Postmodern Use*, 30.

87. Augustine, *OCD* 3.10.14; 3.12.18.

88. See C. H. Dodd, *The Parables of the Kingdom* (New York: Charles Scribner's Sons, 1961), 1. See also McKnight, *Postmodern Use*, 30.

89. See G. Ernest Wright, *The Old Testament and Theology* (New York: Harper & Row, 1969). Wright's limitation in understanding God's work in history deeply enough was, I believe, related to his rejection of incarnational theology which he claimed tended towards "christomonism" (14). He criticized both Karl Barth and Rudolf Bultmann for placing too much emphasis on God's revelation in Jesus. It is obvious from his criticism, however, that he had not given careful attention to Barth's theology. Anyone who has spent time reading Barth's *Church Dogmatics* could not invoke the doctrine of the Trinity, with which Barth structured his whole project, as an element that needs greater consideration (13, 26). Neither could one criticize as Barthian a theology that has no background in the Old Testament and claims that God's revelation is restricted only to the appearance of Jesus (26-27).

90. See Charlesworth, *Jesus Within Judaism*, 10. He is citing Hugh Anderson, *Jesus and Christian Origins* (New York: Oxford University Press, 1964), 307.

91. Gotthold Lessing, "On the Proof of the Spirit and of Power," in *The Shaping of Modern Christian Thought*, eds. Warren F. Grof and Donald E. Miller (New York: World Publishing Co., 1968), 39, 36.

92. See Søren Kierkegaard, *Philosophical Fragments*, trans. David F. Swenson (Princeton: Princeton University Press, 1962), 72-88.

93. See, for instance, Charlesworth, *Jesus Within Judaism*, 26.

94. Flannery O'Connor, "A Good Man is Hard to Find," *Three* (New York: Signet), 142.

INDEX